BIG&GREEN

BIG & GREEN

TOWARD SUSTAINABLE ARCHITECTURE IN THE 21ST CENTURY

EDITED BY DAVID GISSEN

PRINCETON ARCHITECTURAL PRESS | NEW YORK
NATIONAL BUILDING MUSEUM | WASHINGTON, DC

This book is published in conjunction with the exhibition "Big & Green: Toward Sustainable Architecture in the 21st Century," presented at the National Building Museum, Washington, DC, January 17–June 22, 2003.

CURATOR: David Gissen
DIRECTOR OF EXHIBITIONS: Catherine Frankel
CURATORIAL ASSOCIATE: Alisa Goetz
TECHNICAL ADVISOR: Ashok Raiji
CATALOG DESIGN: Paul Carlos and Urshula Barbour, Pure+Applied
EXHIBITION DESIGN: James Hicks and Pure+Applied

This publication is generously supported by the Graham Foundation for Advanced Studies in the Fine Arts.

The exhibition is made possible by:

PATRONS

Jeffrey and Rona Abramson
    and the Abramson Family Foundation

 The Durst Organization

 United States Department of Energy
    Office of Energy Efficiency and
    Renewable Energy

 United States General Services
    Administration Public Buildings Service

SUPPORTERS

Johnson Controls Foundation
Kohn Pedersen Fox Associates, P.C.
Miller & Long Co., Inc.
Turner Construction Company

CONTRIBUTORS

Jones Lang LaSalle Americas
Perkins & Will

FRIENDS

ARUP Services Ltd.
Boggs & Partners
EDAW Inc.
Fox & Fowle Architects
Gannett Co., Inc.
Gensler Family Foundation
Hellmuth, Obata + Kassabaum, Inc.
Montgomery Land Development, Inc.
PEI COBB FREED + PARTNERS Architects, L.L.P.
Cesar Pelli & Associates
Moshe Safdie and Associates, Inc.
SIGAL Construction Corporation
SmithGroup, Inc.

ASSOCIATES

The Clark Construction Group, Inc.
Croxton Collaborative, Architects
Envision Design, P.L.L.C.
Kishimoto.Gordon P.C. Architecture
Utility Systems Construction & Engineering, L.L.C.

DONORS

Kiss + Cathcart Architects
Carl M. Hensler Consulting Services Co.
Maryland Applicators, Inc.
MCLA, Inc.
Morphosis Architects
Smislova, Kehnemui & Associates, P.A.
TOLK, Inc.

(as of July 15, 2002)

Published by
Princeton Architectural Press
37 East Seventh Street
New York, NY 10003
and
National Building Museum
401 F Street NW
Washington, DC 20001

For a free catalog of books, call 1.800.722.6657.
Visit our web site at www.papress.com.

©2002 Princeton Architectural Press
All rights reserved
Printed and bound in China
05 04 03 02   5 4 3 2 1 First edition

Every reasonable attempt has been made to identify owners of copyright. Errors or omissions will be corrected in subsequent editions.

Project coordinator: Mark Lamster
Project editor: Noel Millea

Special thanks: Nettie Aljian, Ann Alter, Nicola Bednarek, Janet Behning, Megan Carey, Penny Chu, Russell Fernandez, Clare Jacobson, Nancy Eklund Later, Linda Lee, Jane Sheinman, Katharine Smalley, Scott Tennent, and Jennifer Thompson of Princeton Architectural Press— Kevin C. Lippert, publisher

Library of Congress
Cataloging-in-Publication Data
Big and green : toward sustainable architecture in the twenty-first century / edited by David Gissen
        p. cm.
    Accompanies an exhibition at the National Building Museum in Washington, DC.
    ISBN 1-56898-361-1 (alk. paper)
    1. Sustainable architecture—Forecasting—Exhibitions. 2. Commercial buildings—Forecasting—Exhibitions. I. Gissen, David. II. National Building Museum (U.S.).
    NA2542.36.B54 2003
    720'.47'074753—dc21
            2002010635

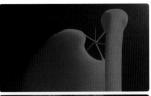

Foreword
by Susan Henshaw Jones

Susan Henshaw Jones is the president of the
National Building Museum.

Like much of the world, the United States is currently experiencing intense growth, especially in and around its cities. Unfortunately, the development that such growth entails is often at odds with the natural environment. As more forest and prairie lands give way to suburban houses and strip malls, the ecological balance of our nation's exurban and rural areas becomes increasingly precarious. Meanwhile, in urban and older suburban areas, commuting time — and, by extension, the consumption of fossil fuels — increases, and precious public space dwindles as more land is devoted to highways and parking lots accommodating the growing crush of traffic.

Any viable solutions to these problems must be conceived in the broadest possible way. While many design and construction professionals have been working for years to create environmentally conscious buildings, for the most part the fruits of their efforts have been relatively small-scale structures and other projects of limited scope. Most modern development is large-scale, however — mixed-use urban complexes, shopping centers, office parks, and so on — and it is in this realm that environmentally conscious building practices can have the greatest impact.

Big & Green: Toward Sustainable Architecture in the 21st Century, published in conjunction with a National Building Museum exhibition of the same name, presents possible solutions to this challenge by documenting cutting-edge practices in large-scale sustainable design. By finding ways to create buildings that consume less energy in their day-to-day operation, use renewable materials, and rely on natural means to ventilate and illuminate their interiors, among many other strategies, architects, engineers, and builders are bringing us closer to the goal of true sustainability.

Some of the essays in *Big & Green* remind us that we might look to buildings in the distant past for ideas about how to build in the future. Indeed, before the advent of air-conditioning and other technologies we now take for granted, architects and builders had no choice but to create sustainable structures. The home of the National Building Museum is one example: Designed by Montgomery C. Meigs and completed in 1887 to house the U.S. Pension Bureau, it was one of the largest office buildings of its time and featured operable windows and skylights that provided its occupants access to sunlight and air-circulation year-round. It is interesting to note that over 100 years later, several municipal governments have introduced legislation to require that employees' workstations be located within a certain distance of an operable window.

During work on the exhibition, the terrible events of September 11 caused us to reconsider our project and its significance in light of the debates over the skyscraper and other dense forms of development. We believe the exhibition is stronger and even more relevant given recent world events, and hope that it will provide useful ideas as we begin the process of rebuilding in the wake of the terrorist attacks.

The fund-raising efforts for "Big & Green" were led by museum trustee Jeffrey S. Abramson of the Tower Companies, a Washington-area developer with a strong commitment to sustainable design and construction. A. Eugene Kohn of the architecture firm Kohn Pedersen Fox Associates in New York also provided important fund-raising leadership. This catalog was supported by a generous grant from the Graham Foundation for Advanced Studies in the Fine Arts. Significant funding for the project was provided by Jeffrey and Rona Abramson and the Abramson Family Foundation, the Durst Organization, the U.S. Department of Energy, and the U.S. General Services Administration. Major support was also provided by the Johnson Controls Foundation, Kohn Pedersen Fox Associates, P.C., Miller & Long Co., Inc., and the Turner Construction Company. I thank them, along with all of the other funders who made this project possible.

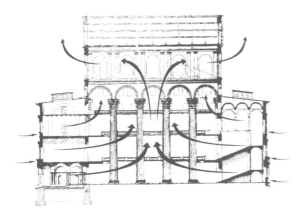

This exhibition and catalog are the creations of a dedicated team at the National Building Museum who have worked for the past two and a half years, gathering over 50 international projects into the most comprehensive exhibition of contemporary sustainable architecture to date. The curator of the exhibition was David Gissen, who led the exhibition team under the active guidance of chief curator Howard Decker. Other key participants included director of exhibitions Catherine Frankel and curatorial associate Alisa Goetz. Ashok Raiji of ARUP Services Ltd. was the exhibition's technical advisor and brought a sophisticated knowledge of environmental systems and sustainable building practices to the curatorial team. We are indebted to Ashok, whose contributions have been invaluable. This team was assisted by the energetic work of Armand Graham and student interns Charlotte Barrows and Yvonne Zaragoza.

An exhibition advisory committee was formed to counsel the team on broad trends and technical details of sustainable architecture and to review the content of the exhibition and catalog. Exhibition cochairs Jeffrey Abramson, Douglas Durst, and Eugene Kohn led the committee, which included Betty Arndt, William Browning, Randall Croxton, Bruce Fowle, Robert Fox, Kriz Kizak Wines, William McDonough, William Odell, Ashok Raiji, Gerald Sigal, Paul von Paumgartten, Kendall Wilson, and James Wines. We are grateful for their assistance.

This catalog and the exhibition it accompanies highlight some of the most recent representative projects and the most passionate advocates for large-scale sustainable architecture. The buildings on these pages are unlike other skyscrapers, apartment buildings, or large commercial developments; they feature rooftop gardens, solar panels, wind turbines, and recycled and renewable materials, among numerous other environmentally conscious features. The essays explain how government and city leaders, developers, architects, engineers, and builders can collaborate to remake existing buildings and create new structures that support the environment. As making big buildings green becomes standard practice, this catalog will serve as the historical record of the theoretical and practical foundations of large-scale sustainable design.

Preface
by William McDonough

William McDonough is the founding principal of William McDonough + Partners and cofounder of McDonough Braungart Design Chemistry.

As the twentieth century came to a close, most new buildings had become so divorced from their surroundings that the *Wall Street Journal* devoted an entire front-page feature to a new office building designed by my firm, because it had windows that could actually be opened.[1] When operable windows make news for setting a design standard, we have reached an astonishingly low point in architecture. Could we be any further from an architecture that sustains us and connects us with the natural world? Perhaps not. But under the radar of architectural fashion and the popular press, architects have been busy working out the elements of a much richer concept of sustainable building design.

What Is Sustainability?

A growing awareness of the environmental, social, and economic problems associated with contemporary architecture and industry has led many business leaders and communities to adopt practices deemed to be more sustainable over the long term. Such strategies are usually aimed at keeping the engines of commerce humming and people employed, while reducing resource consumption, energy use, toxic emissions, and waste. The result is that the sustainability agenda tends to be a framework for the reform of the existing industrial system rather than a fundamental redesign, a way of being "less bad" by being more efficient. Most architects who are sensitive to sustainability issues try to do more with less by designing buildings that make more efficient use of energy and resources. But is being less bad the same thing as being good? Does mere efficiency meet our need to connect with the natural world or does it just slow down ecological destruction? And if sustainable architecture falls short of fulfilling our needs, what would a *sustaining* architecture look like?

Architecture and Nature's Laws

We could begin to look for answers in the natural world: Nature is a source of both sustenance and exquisite design. The Earth's natural communities are extraordinarily effective at making food from the sun, producing oxygen, filtering water, and recycling nutrients and energy. Yet natural communities are not particularly efficient. They are fertile, regenerative, complex, responsive, profligate, and extravagant — what some might call wasteful. They thrive not by reproducing the same response worldwide but by fitting elegantly into a profusion of niches. Even nature's laws express themselves variously in different communities, as processes such as photosynthesis and nutrient cycling yield different forms from region to region. We could say form doesn't just follow function, it follows evolution. This delightful confluence of the unique and the universal suggests the lineaments of a new theory of architecture for a fast-growing world. Perhaps, instead of only following the law of gravity, architects could follow other natural laws that govern evolving life: One organism's waste equals food for another; living things thrive on the energy of the sun; and natural systems celebrate diversity.

Design and the Celebration of Life

Most conventional practitioners of modern design and

1. Neal Templin, "Windows That Open Are the Latest Office Amenity," *Wall Street Journal,* August 26, 1998.

computer renderings,
Museum of Life and the
Environment, York County,
South Carolina, William
McDonough + Partners,
2001—

remains a vital idea. With clarity of mind and intention, architects can begin to understand the complex nature of a particular building in a particular evolutionary matrix in a particular place in the world. Form can become a celebration not simply of human intelligence but of our kinship with all of life.

From Dominion to Kinship

The buildings in this exhibition and catalog are more than just examples of the technological bells and whistles of green design. They are part of an evolving cultural phenomenon. They seek to replace dominion over nature with a more fulfilling relationship with the natural world. This movement away from dominion, past simple stewardship, and toward a sense of kinship—what the great biologist E.O. Wilson calls "biophilia"—is a source of creativity and compassion, wonder and hope. If this century is to be known for peace, prosperity, beauty, and the restoration of our world, kinship with nature must become one of the foundations of our cultural life. And architecture, with its profound ability to create new relationships to place, is uniquely positioned to lead such a renaissance.

construction find it easier to make buildings as if nature and place did not exist. In Rangoon or Racine, their work is the same. Fossil fuels make buildings in both locales inhabitable, lighting them, cooling them, heating them. An ecologically aware architect would design those buildings differently. She would immerse herself in the life of each place, tapping into natural and cultural history, investigating local energy sources, the availability of sunlight, shade, and water, the vernacular architecture of the region, the lives of local birds, trees, and grasses. Her intention would be to design a building that creates aesthetic, economic, social, and ecological values for the surrounding human and natural communities—more positive effects, not fewer negative ones. This would represent an entirely new approach: Following nature's laws, one might discover that form follows celebration.

While Sullivan declared Form Follows Function to clarify architectural intention, he also went on to explore and celebrate in ornament the life-forms evolved from a seed. Mies, with his famous maxim, Less Is More, went still further to unclutter architectural theory and practice. The buildings of Mies's less ambitious followers may lack elegance in their relation to place, but the practice of paring away to arrive at the essence of form

With "Big & Green," the National Building Museum explores this relationship between the things we build and the places we inhabit. The buildings featured in the exhibition represent small steps toward an ideal. They capture a moment in which we are striving to find a new way of living. None of the problems associated with large-scale building design has been solved; many issues remain to be addressed. But this exhibition offers clues, a suggestion of possibilities. There are hints of an abundant future, a new engagement with the natural world, and better, more enriching places—by design. These intimations suggest that what some might see as our tragic relationship with nature in the last century could well be transformed into a more hopeful one as we enter the heart of the next.

9

Introduction
by David Gissen

"Green," or environmentally responsible, architecture burst onto the international scene in the 1970s in response to visible evidence of environmental damage and rising fuel prices. The first green architects focused primarily on single-family homes, although some promising work was done on office buildings. In the ensuing years, however, architects interested in environmental issues have increasingly directed their efforts at skyscrapers, apartment buildings, convention centers, shopping complexes, and other large-scale commercial buildings, which according to their research consume enormous amounts of energy, release large amounts of carbon dioxide, use the most wasteful construction techniques, and have poor air quality that can cause numerous illnesses. "Big & Green" examines the technological systems and design strategies of a new generation of environmentally sensitive, large-scale buildings and locates this work historically through examinations of similar buildings from the past.

Early Passive Environments
In the late nineteenth century—before electrical heating, cooling, and illumination—architects used a combination of mechanical

devices and "passive" techniques (which worked without electrical or mechanical equipment) to illuminate and ventilate the interior spaces of high-rise and long-span buildings. Many large buildings, especially skyscrapers, used mechanical ventilation equipment and relied on steam systems for heating. Cooling and illumination, though, were usually achieved through passive means: The designers of early gallerias and factories often devised ingenious systems to remove hot air and introduce cooler air, and the designers of early skyscrapers tempered the heat of the summer sun by setting windows deep into the facade, where they were shaded.[1]

The design for the first *New York Times* Building (Eidlitz & McKenzie, 1905), for example, featured deep-set windows at the top to help shield the most exposed portion of the building from the sun. Similar strategies were evident in other buildings of the pre-air-conditioning era. The Flatiron Building (D.H. Burnham & Company, 1903), another structure with an unprecedented degree of solar exposure, had windows set deep in its thermally absorbent stone skin, and many of Louis Sullivan's structures had integrated retractable awnings that presaged the current use of smart skins. These awnings were a common in the new glass-and-steel architecture.[2]

Architects recognized the problems of ventilation created by buildings whose ceilings and floors (the traditional place for air-extraction) were above and below numerous other floors—as well as the problems created simply by these buildings' unprecedented scale. Traditionally, long-span sheds used for train stations and exhibition spaces—such as Joseph Paxton's famous Crystal Palace (1851)—contained ventilators on the peaks of the roofs. The designer of the Galleria Vittorio Emanuele II (1877), Giuseppe Mengoni, developed a more artful solution for ventilating the long-span space. It featured what is today called a labyrinth: Air was pulled into underground chambers where it was cooled by the earth and then returned through vents in the floor as needed.[3]

Mechanical Environments

By World War II, most mid-rise and high-rise buildings used an impressive array of passive strategies. In Manhattan's Rockefeller Center (Hood and Corbett, 1932), for example, workers had access to sky gardens, and their work spaces were within 27 feet of operable windows recessed into a stone skin, which allowed them to have direct control over their immediate environment. Despite

1. Stefan and Sofia Behling, *Solar Power: The Evolution of Sustainable Architecture* (New York: Prestel, 2000) and Reyner Banham, *The Architecture of the Well-Tempered Environment* (London: Architectural P., 1969).

2. For one of the few published images of the Wainwright Building that shows awnings, see Dell Upton, *Architecture in the United States* (New York: Oxford University Press, 1998), 143–44, 214. Unfortunately, almost all twentieth-century architectural histories favor a "pure," or non-environmental, understanding of these early high-rises—thus the summer photographs of the Wainwright Building, the Guaranty Building, and the Carson Pirie & Scott Department Store that clearly show sunshading awnings have remained mostly unpublished.

3. Stefan and Sofia Behling, *Solar Power*.

these achievements, most architects and engineers in the subsequent postwar era were more interested in figuring out how to incorporate air-conditioning into the tall building and the new long-span spaces of mall complexes than in making those buildings responsive to their surroundings.

As architects explored the potential of air-conditioning, they developed a new form for high-rise, mid-rise, and long-span spaces that reflected this move away from passive strategies. These buildings featured an entirely new language of smooth-skinned glass-and-steel boxes without operable windows, ventilators, or external sunshades. And with the development of low-wattage fluorescent lights that didn't emit much heat, the floor area of these structures was widened to the point where natural illumination was replaced completely with artificial.

The affordability of these new buildings and the fossil fuels used to drive the generators that powered them explains, in large part, why passive environmental control was phased out. Of course, air-conditioning also provided comfort in the summer, an issue that future environmentally conscious architects would have to address with more aggressive strategies to cool buildings passively.[4]

Energy-Efficient Environments

Despite widespread acceptance of this new approach to building, a number of economic and ecological crises in the 1960s and 1970s led to a reexamination of energy use in buildings and a rediscovery of passive strategies. This coincided with a popular environmental movement reflected in best-selling books such as *Silent Spring* by Rachel Carson (1962) and public demonstrations such as the first Earth Day in 1970. Public concern about environmental issues only grew with the oil crisis of 1973, the result of an Arab response to Western aid to Israel during the Yom Kippur War, which culminated in a decision by OPEC (the Organization of Petroleum Exporting Countries) to drastically reduce oil production. When the cost of operating heating and cooling systems increased exponentially, U.S. and Western European government researchers focused on reducing energy consumption in commercial buildings and single-family homes, which was estimated to account for almost 40 percent of energy consumption worldwide.[5]

Among the most innovative energy-efficient buildings in the United States at the time were eight state office buildings commissioned by the Jerry Brown administration in California in the late

FAR LEFT **Gregory Bateson Building, Office of the State Architect, Sacramento, California, 1978**
LEFT **interior of Bateson Building showing canvas air distributor**
OPPOSITE **view of green roof and glass wall, Willis Faber and Dumas Headquarters, Ipswich, England, Foster and Partners, 1977**

4. Banham, *Well-Tempered Environment*.

5. David Lloyd Jones, *Architecture and the Environment: Bioclimatic Building Design* (London: Laurence King, 1998), 47–48.

1970s. The best known, the Gregory Bateson Building in Sacramento (1978), was designed by Sim van der Ryn, Office of the State Architect. It incorporated advanced passive heating and cooling strategies such as rocks under the first floor called "rock stores," which held cool air and released it into office spaces, and energy-generating equipment, such as photovoltaics, on the roof. In the office spaces, workers were seated in groups of 20 or 30, and each group was able to control the climate in its section of the building. Although many of the technologies did not work as expected, the Bateson Building and the other structures designed by Van der Ryn remain an important milestone in the development of environmentally sensitive offices in the United States.[6]

In Europe, where the price of energy was even higher, governments encouraged architects, engineers, and builders to develop strategies to naturally illuminate, ventilate, and supply power to buildings. English architects such as Alexander Pike, Richard Rogers, and Norman Foster responded to this new desire for energy efficiency with luminous, well-ventilated, prefabricated large-scale buildings. These architects incorporated ideas from earlier, passive buildings, from Buckminster Fuller (prefabrication and

technological imagery), and from the emerging aerospace industry (solar cells, wind turbines, and mirrored glass).

One of the most environmentally progressive British projects was the Willis Faber and Dumas Headquarters (Foster and Partners, 1977), which has been cited as a pivotal building in recent histories of the origins of sustainable architecture. According to critics such as Ed Melet, one of the major accomplishments of this project—and the high-tech movement in general—was that it showed that energy-efficient, environmentally sensitive architecture *could* be built if advanced technology was combined with passive techniques. The Headquarters' glass wall was fixed, like that of any postwar office building, but the inoperable windows were mirrored, reducing heat gain while providing large amounts of daylight, and a large atrium increased natural illumination. The Willis Faber and Dumas Headquarters also featured a grass roof, which kept the floors beneath it cool and provided an opportunity for workers to interact with nature. Although the building would not, by today's standards, be considered environmentally sensitive—it is fully serviced by an air-conditioning plant and does not contain operable windows—it proved that environmentalist

6. Upton, *Architecture in the United States*, 143–44.

13

goals could be realized in corporate office buildings.[7]

Healthy Environments

The greening of large-scale buildings gained momentum in the mid-1980s, when the American architect William McDonough, who had built a career developing self-sufficient solar homes and communities, began publicly voicing his concerns about the toxicity of the materials used in commercial buildings. McDonough was the most vocal of a group of East Coast architecture firms, including the Croxton Collaborative and Fox & Fowle Architects, who attacked American building practices and encouraged architects and builders to reexamine the construction materials and air systems used in office buildings. William McDonough + Partners' investigations into construction materials and the Croxton Collaborative's research into air quality were primarily responsible for the new focus on physiological issues in environmentally sensitive architecture. At a time when fuel costs were no longer exorbitant, these issues gave a renewed purpose to the environmental movement in architecture.

William McDonough + Partners' early materials research centered on the off-gassing of materials in office interiors. "Off-gassing"

refers to chemical vapors released into the air during construction and, over time, by the construction materials themselves (which include fabrics, plywoods, and paints). During renovation of the Environmental Defense Fund office, William McDonough + Partners was asked by the client to find out which material compounds were being used to manufacture the interior materials. In reaction to his findings, McDonough developed new carpets from plants and specified woods devoid of chemicals to be used in the project. This appreciation for nontoxic materials has now become one of the tenets of green design.

Architects in other parts of the world were simultaneously exploring new environmentally sensitive practices to improve energy efficiency, air quality, and occupant health. The German architect Thomas Herzog of Herzog + Partner was an early pioneer of prefabricated, energy-efficient window and wall systems. In his native Malaysia, Kenneth Yeang and his firm T.R. Hamzah and Yeang developed techniques to incorporate sky gardens and water-reclamation systems in skyscrapers. They and the rest of these groundbreaking architecture firms—Sim van der Ryn, Richard Rogers Partnership, Foster and Partners, William McDonough + Partners, Croxton

7. Ed Melet, *Sustainable Architecture: Towards a Diverse Built Environment* (Rotterdam: NAI Publishers, 1999).

Collaborative, and Fox & Fowle—laid the foundations for exploring large-scale environmentally sensitive building techniques, and many remain the leaders in research and application today.

Sustainable Environments

By the 1990s, European and American architects interested in environmentally sensitive architecture supported a theoretical concept they called "sustainable development" or, more commonly, "sustainability." Sustainable development was defined by the United Nations' World Commission on Environment and Development in the 1987 "Bruntland Report" (after the then–prime minister of Norway, Gro Harlem Bruntland), as development that "meets the needs of the present without compromising the ability of future generations to meet their own needs."

While no simple list can cover all the requirements large-scale buildings must meet in order to be considered sustainable— especially as scientists continue to evaluate the environmental impact of these structures—there are now a number of rating systems used to evaluate sustainable architecture in general terms. LEED (Leadership in Energy and Environmental Design) and

BREEAM (Building Research Establishment Environmental Assessment Method) both rate buildings according to their environmental impact. Each system reflects the concerns of a particular culture, but they both address the issues that first catalyzed the environmental movement in the 1970s. They define environmentally progressive architecture as an architecture that uses renewable sources to generate energy; that uses passive techniques for ventilation and illumination; that incorporates, maintains, and recycles greenery, water, and waste; that advances the use of environmentally conscious construction techniques; and that fosters a livable and viable urbanism.

The essays and descriptions of projects assembled in this catalog explore the ways in which these criteria are transforming large-scale commercial building. In "The Air We Breathe," Guy Battle discusses renewable energy systems and the light and air systems used in today's large-scale buildings. In "Vertiscapes," James Wines examines the historic and contemporary use of greenery in skyscrapers. Michael Braungart examines sustainability from the point of view of construction practices and materials, and David Serlin looks at the need for social sustainability

RIGHT **Condé Nast Building at Four Times Square, New York City, Fox & Fowle Architects, 1999**

OPPOSITE LEFT **Commerzbank, Frankfurt, Germany, Foster and Partners, 1996**

OPPOSITE RIGHT **Dutch Pavilion, Expo 2000, Hannover, Germany, MVRDV, 2000**

in contemporary office buildings. Finally, Nina Rappaport and Ashok Raiji synthesize these concerns in interviews with leading architects and a glossary of sustainable building terms. Illustrations and descriptions provide thorough documentation of the technological systems and environmentally sensitive components of 50 projects. Each building is evaluated according to its use of energy-generating technology; light and air systems; greenery, water, and waste systems; construction systems; and urban planning.

Some of the most visible and influential new environmentally sensitive buildings are large-scale structures—the Audubon House by the Croxton Collaborative, Lloyd's of London by Richard Rogers Partnership, Four Times Square by Fox & Fowle, and the Commerzbank by Foster and Partners. With the completion of these works, it's clear that large-scale commercial architecture *can* be environmentally sensitive. The American Institute of Architects' Committee on the Environment's annual list of top green buildings includes a growing number of commercial buildings over 100,000 square feet, and many of the sustainable projects currently in development around the world will be the largest structures ever built in their respective cities.

Designers such as MVRDV, SITE, and T.R. Hamzah and Yeang express the new scale of sustainable technologies by imagining entirely new types of living and working environments that feature multilevel gardens, amorphous shapes, and high-tech imagery. Other firms such as Robert A.M. Stern Architects, Cesar Pelli & Associates, and HOK incorporate sustainable technologies more discreetly, without any noticeable change in the exterior or interior environment. Despite these aesthetic differences, all of the projects in this exhibition share a commitment to the environment, technology, and design—and all search for an architecture that can be both big *and* green.

David Gissen is the curator of architecture and design at the National Building Museum and an instructor in architecture and design theory at the American University, the Maryland Institute College of Art, and most recently, Pennsylvania State University.

ENERGY

Each of the projects on the following pages, selected by the National Building Museum to be part of "Big & Green," is categorized according to: BUILDING TYPE (low-rise, mid-rise, high-rise, or long-span); ENERGY GENERATION (use of renewable energy sources and ability to conserve and generate energy); LIGHT & AIR (use of passive systems for illumination and ventilation); GREENERY, WATER & WASTE (use of landscaping, water conservation and reuse, and recycling); CONSTRUCTION (use of renewable, nontoxic materials and strategies for limiting the pollution generated during construction); and URBANISM (attention paid to siting and environmental planning issues).

The consumption of fossil fuels is one of our biggest environmental problems. Drilling in ecologically sensitive areas, oil spills, air pollution, and the destruction of the atmosphere all result from the incredible demand for fossil fuels. We may think of cars and factories as the most obvious enemies of the environment, but buildings consume more than half the energy used worldwide. Mechanical systems that supply air-conditioning and heating, lighting systems, and other building technologies are now being redesigned to consume less energy—and, most important, alternate sources of energy are being developed. While building owners can purchase energy made from renewable or clean sources (solar, wind, or hydroelectric), many architects are now designing buildings that generate their own clean and renewable energy. If this trend continues, future architects may develop buildings that generate all their own power, with enough left over to contribute to the city's power supply.

The Ventiform research project was an attempt to integrate an electricity-generating wind turbine into a mixed-use, high-rise building. Its name was inspired by ventifacts, rocks that are carved into aerodynamic forms by windblown sand. The building uses the Enercon E66 wind turbine, also designed by Foster and Partners, which generates enough clean, renewable energy to power 1,500 suburban homes. The aerodynamic form of the building enhances the energy-generating capability of the turbine, increasing the building's self-sufficiency.

RIGHT **airflow diagrams**

ARCHITECT
Foster and Partners

YEAR
2001 (unbuilt)

BUILDING TYPE
- high-rise

ENERGY GENERATION
- renewable energy use
- energy conservation systems

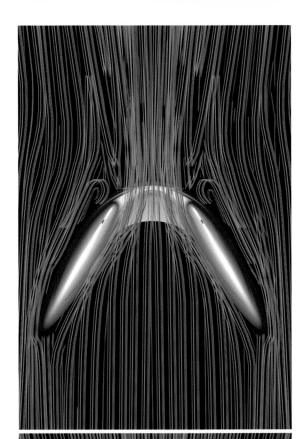

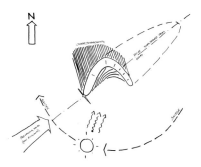

LEFT **sketches showing potential orientation of tower**

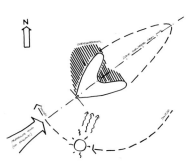

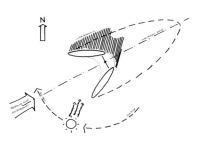

OPPOSITE **views of model showing integrated wind turbine**

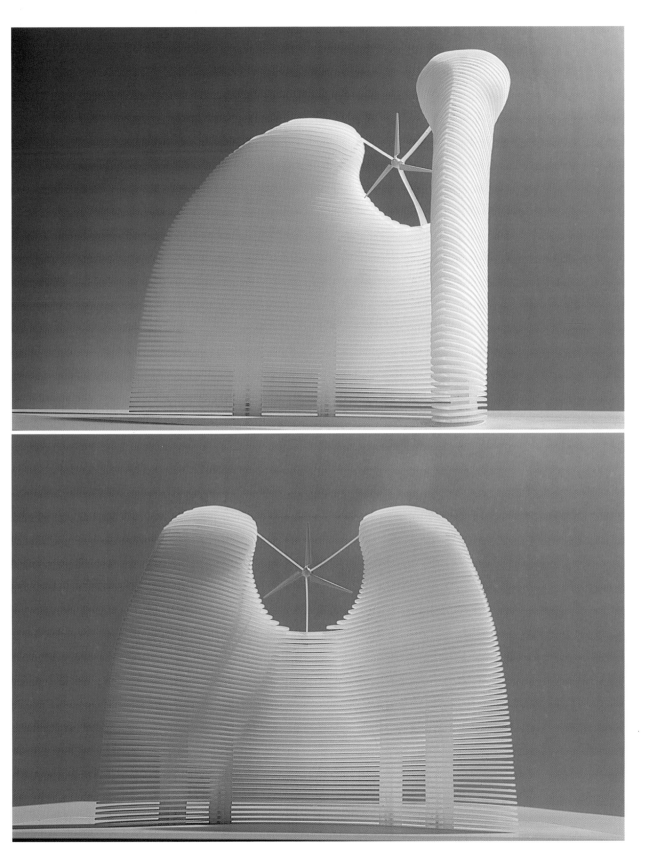

02.

All of Four Times Square's building systems and construction technologies were evaluated for their environmental sensitivity, their effect on occupant health, and their ability to reduce energy consumption, making this the largest building in the United States to establish standards for energy conservation, indoor air quality, recycling systems, and sustainable manufacturing processes. The building uses environmentally efficient gas-fired absorption chillers and a state-of-the-art curtain wall, which provides shading and insulation. The air delivery system provides 50 percent more fresh air than industry codes require, and a network of recycling chutes serves the entire building. Stringent procedures were followed during construction and continue to be followed in the day-to-day operations of the building in order to maintain these standards.

ARCHITECT
Fox & Fowle
Architects

LOCATION
New York City

YEAR
1999

CLIENT
The Durst Organization

STRUCTURAL ENGINEER
Cantor Seinuk Group

MECHANICAL ENGINEER
Cosentini Associates

CONSTRUCTION MANAGER
Tishman Construction
Corporation

BUILDING TYPE
- high-rise

ENERGY GENERATION
- renewable energy use
- energy conservation systems

LIGHT & AIR
- daylight illumination
- monitored air quality

GREENERY, WATER & WASTE
- water conservation and reuse
- building recycling program

CONSTRUCTION
- use of renewable materials
- use of local or regional materials
- modular construction techniques

URBANISM
- public transportation access
- site reuse

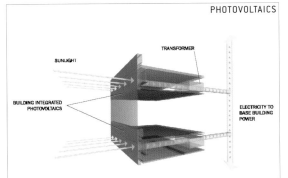

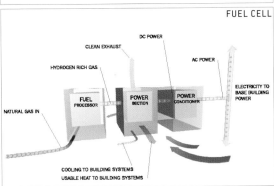

OPPOSITE **view of building at night showing integrated photovoltaic cells on facade**   ABOVE **diagrams showing energy-generating technologies**

ABOVE **view of building entrance**

The new Reuters Building at Seventh Avenue and 42nd Street occupies a prominent position in New York City's Times Square. The building was designed to accommodate energy-generating fuel cells and photovoltaic panels in the glass-skin curtain wall. When these technologies are eventually implemented, the Reuters Building will be one of the two largest environmentally sensitive buildings in the United States, along with the Condé Nast Building. As built, it contains glass that reduces the buildup of heat from the sun while allowing for optimal daylighting, as well as dual-fired absorption chillers for air-conditioning and occupancy sensors in the fire stairs and maintenance rooms.

ARCHITECT
Fox & Fowle Architects

LOCATION
New York City

YEAR
2001

CLIENT
Three Times Square Associates, L.L.C.

BUILDING SERVICES ENGINEER
Jaros, Baum & Bolles Consulting Engineers

STRUCTURAL ENGINEER
Severud Associates

CONSTRUCTION MANAGER
Tishman Construction Corporation

BUILDING TYPE
- high-rise

ENERGY GENERATION
- energy conservation systems

LIGHT & AIR
- daylight illumination
- monitored air quality

GREENERY, WATER & WASTE
- water conservation and reuse
- building recycling program

CONSTRUCTION
- use of renewable materials
- use of local or regional materials
- modular construction techniques

URBANISM
- public transportation access
- site reuse

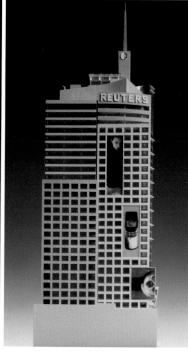

ABOVE **views of model**

LEFT **section drawing**

OPPOSITE **view of building showing window variation**

ABOVE **computer rendering of photovoltaic facade**

04. PROJECT
HEW Customer Center

When the aging facade of its customer center in Hamburg's central shopping district needed to be replaced, HEW—Hamburg's electrical utility and one of Europe's foremost proponents of solar energy—hired Kiss + Cathcart to provide an energy- and resource-efficient solution. The architects draped a photovoltaic glass skin over the existing building to insulate it against moisture and temperature extremes. In front of the building, the glass skin pulls away to envelop a first-floor winter garden and a street-front cafe. The photovoltaic second skin not only eliminated the need to demolish and dispose of the existing facade, reducing environmental damage, it also generates electricity and heat year-round.

ARCHITECT
Kiss + Cathcart Architects

ASSOCIATE ARCHITECT
Sommer + Partner,
Architects

LOCATION
Hamburg, Germany

YEAR
1999 [unbuilt]

CLIENT:
Hamburgische
Electricitäts-Werke AG

ENGINEER
ARUP Services Ltd.

BUILDING TYPE
● mid-rise

ENERGY GENERATION
● renewable energy use
● energy conservation systems

LIGHT & AIR
● daylight illumination
● natural ventilation systems

CONSTRUCTION
● modular construction
  techniques
● building reuse

URBANISM
● environmental planning
● public transportation access
● site reuse

ABOVE **computer rendering of outdoor seating area**

BELOW **axonometric drawings of photovoltaic facade and supporting structure**

RIGHT **diagrams of energy-generation and ventilation strategies**

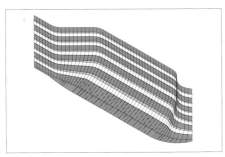

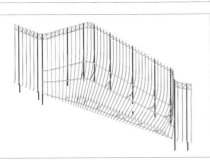

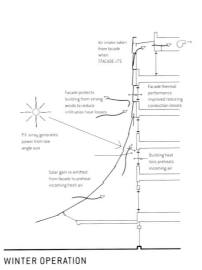

Air intake taken from facade when TFACADE >TS

Facade protects building from strong winds to reduce infiltration heat losses

Facade thermal performance improved reducing conduction losses

P.V. array generates power from low angle sun

Building heat loss preheats incoming air

Solar gain re-emitted from facade to preheat incoming fresh air

WINTER OPERATION

Hot air vents directly to outside when TFACADE >TS

Fresh air intake direct from outside

Double facade penetrated by intermediate operable windows to allow natural ventilation

Balcony area ventilated directly to outside

Air in facade picks up heat gain from P.V. cells and existing facade and rises due to bouyancy

P.V. arrays provide shading and power generation

Planters provide additional thermal mass

Facade permeable at lower levels allows fresh air to be drawn into atrium

Foliage provides additional shading

SUMMER OPERATION

Designed specifically for "Big & Green," this massive, 150-story mixed-use tower employs a combination of solar and wind power systems, among other sustainable strategies. On either side of the tower, louvered solar panels create a cage that surrounds the wind turbines, reducing the rippling shadows from the turbines and generating enough power to make the building completely energy-independent. Water-reclamation systems and catchments, located at 30-floor intervals, recycle rain and waste water, so the building releases only 10 percent of its waste water into the city's sewage system. There is a hotel on the sixtieth floor, a theater complex on the ninetieth floor, a botanical garden on the hundred-and-twentieth floor, and a museum and viewing space on the hundred-and-fiftieth floor.

ARCHITECT
Kiss + Cathcart Architects

YEAR
2002 (unbuilt)

STRUCTURAL & MECHANICAL ENGINEER
ARUP Services Ltd.

BUILDING TYPE
- high-rise

ENERGY GENERATION
- renewable energy use
- energy exporting

LIGHT & AIR
- daylight illumination
- natural ventilation systems

GREENERY, WATER & WASTE
- interior gardens
- water conservation and reuse

CONSTRUCTION
- modular construction techniques

URBANISM
- environmental planning
- public transportation access
- mixed-use building

ABOVE **computer renderings of public area and sky garden**

RIGHT **section diagram of environmental features**

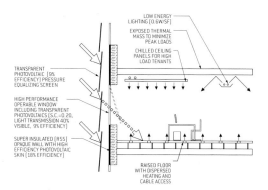

LOW ENERGY LIGHTING (0.6W/SF)

EXPOSED THERMAL MASS TO MINIMIZE PEAK LOADS

CHILLED CEILING PANELS FOR HIGH LOAD TENANTS

TRANSPARENT PHOTOVOLTAIC (9% EFFICIENCY) PRESSURE EQUALIZING SCREEN

HIGH PERFORMANCE OPERABLE WINDOW INCLUDING TRANSPARENT PHOTOVOLTAICS (S.C.=0.20, LIGHT TRANSMISSION 40% VISIBLE, 9% EFFICIENCY)

SUPER INSULATED (R55) OPAQUE WALL WITH HIGH EFFICIENCY PHOTOVOLTAIC SKIN (18% EFFICIENCY)

RAISED FLOOR WITH DISPERSED HEATING AND CABLE ACCESS

RIGHT **computer rendering of tower**

The Centre International Rogier project is a renovation of an existing, technologically innovative tower block from the 1960s. The renovation features low-energy technologies such as ventilated cavity windows, a chilled ceiling system, and energy-generating wind turbines. If this project had been built, it would have been the first skyscraper to incorporate wind turbines. To this day, wind turbines have not been realized in a skyscraper of this size.

ARCHITECT
Kohn Pedersen Fox Associates

LOCATION
Brussels, Belgium

YEAR
1999 [unbuilt]

CLIENT
Brussels Business Centre, S.A.

ASSOCIATE ARCHITECT
Samyn & Partners

STRUCTURAL ENGINEER
ARUP Services Ltd.

MECHANICAL, ELECTRICAL & PLUMBING ENGINEER
Battle McCarthy Consulting Engineers & Landscape Architects

BUILDING TYPE
- high-rise

ENERGY GENERATION
- renewable energy use

LIGHT & AIR
- daylight illumination
- natural ventilation systems
- operable windows

CONSTRUCTION
- modular construction techniques
- use of renewable materials
- building reuse

URBANISM
- environmental planning
- site reuse

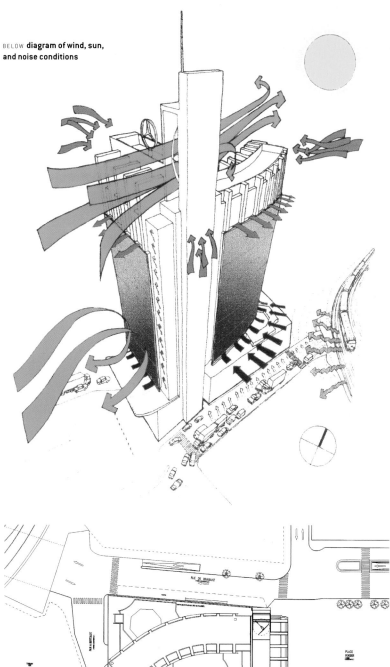

BELOW **diagram of wind, sun, and noise conditions**

RIGHT **site plan**

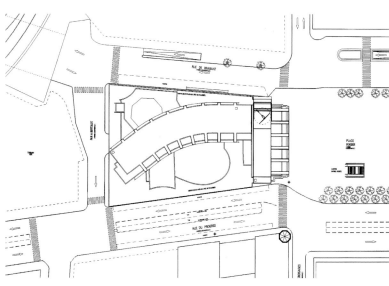

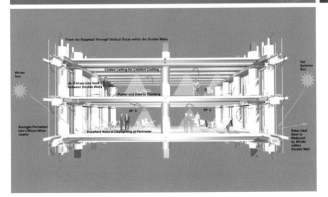

ABOVE **photographs of model showing integrated wind turbines in roof tower**
LEFT **diagram of environmental systems in typical offices**

PROJECT
Jets Stadium

The new Jets Stadium will be a 75,000-seat, open-air stadium and multipurpose facility located on Manhattan's western edge. The architects used a variety of advanced technologies including solar cells and wind turbines, which were integrated into the enormous metal screens at the north and south of the stadium. If built as planned, this will be one of the world's largest energy-generating buildings and the first energy-generating professional sports stadium in the United States. The complex's energy-generating systems will provide power not only to the stadium but to the surrounding city grid as well.

ARCHITECT
Kohn Pedersen Fox Associates

LOCATION
New York City

YEAR
2001–

CLIENT
New York Jets

STRUCTURAL ENGINEER
Thornton Tomasetti Engineers

MECHANICAL, ELECTRICAL & PLUMBING ENGINEER
Flack & Kurtz, Inc.

ENVIRONMENTAL ENGINEER
Battle McCarthy Consulting Engineers & Landscape Architects

SPORTS ARCHITECT
Heinlen Schrock Stearns

BUILDING TYPE
● long-span

ENERGY GENERATION
● renewable energy use
● energy exporting

LIGHT & AIR
● daylight illumination
● natural ventilation systems

GREENERY, WATER & WASTE
● water conservation and reuse

CONSTRUCTION
● modular construction techniques

URBANISM
● environmental planning
● public transportation access
● site reuse

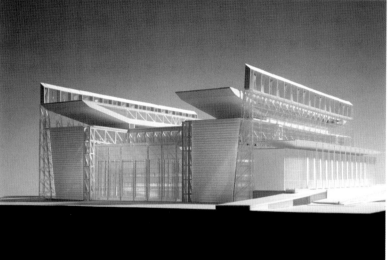

TOP **computer rendering of building in context**

ABOVE **photograph of model showing retractable roof**

OPPOSITE TOP **photomontage of building in context**

OPPOSITE BOTTOM **diagrams of the building's solar and wind power systems**

33

08. PROJECT
Turbine Tower

ARCHITECT
Richard Rogers
Partnership

LOCATION
Tokyo, Japan

YEAR
1992–1993 (unbuilt)

STRUCTURAL & MECHANICAL ENGINEER
ARUP Services Ltd.

Using wind-tunnel visualization to fine-tune the relationship between the main building and its core, the architects designed an aerodynamic form that ventilates the building and facilitates energy generation. The building's shape accelerates natural breezes as they pass through the structure, driving the turbines and generating power. Computer modeling suggests that, if built, the tower would require no additional power.

BUILDING TYPE
● high-rise

ENERGY GENERATION
● renewable energy use
● energy exporting
● energy conservation systems

LIGHT & AIR
● daylight illumination
● natural ventilation systems
● monitored air quality

CONSTRUCTION
● modular construction techniques

URBANISM
● environmental planning

ABOVE **sketch of building, Richard Rogers**

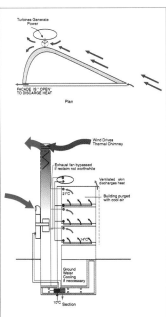

ABOVE **diagrams of ventilation system during summer and winter**

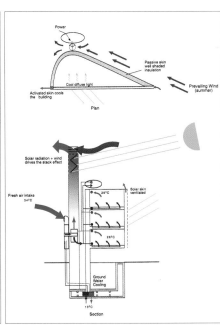

OPPOSITE **photograph of model showing integrated wind turbines between office areas and ventilation tube**

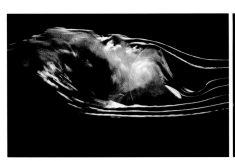

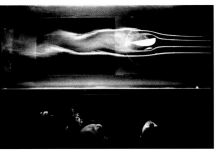

LEFT **photographs of wind tunnel test on building model**

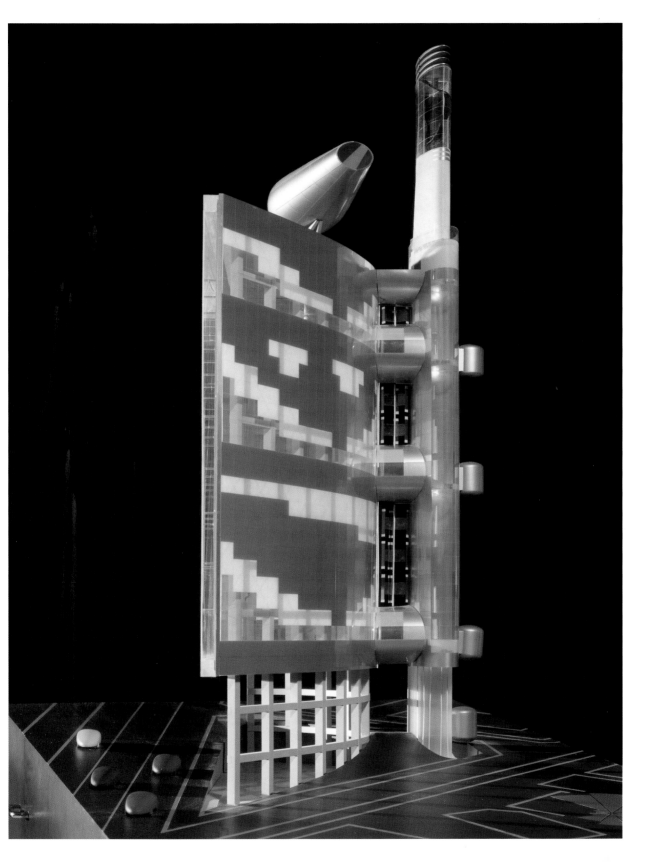

The Air We Breathe

by Guy Battle

"Human history becomes more and more a race between education and catastrophe." H.G. WELLS (1866–1946)

Air is an essential resource for supporting life, a unifying substance for mankind. Every molecule of air we breathe has a 99 percent chance of having been breathed before. Air knows no boundaries or borders, circulating around the Earth in response to temperature and pressure differences and phenomena such as the Coriolis force, created by the rotation of the Earth. But even so, we do not recognize air as a finite resource, and we have not yet developed a sense of responsibility for it. At one point our attitude toward water was similar. However, in the latter part of the twentieth century, with the drought conditions that plague cities worldwide, we developed a greater sense of responsibility for water use. It is now relatively commonplace for European buildings, at least, to recycle the water they use on site. Our attitude toward air is distinctly different: We fail to recognize our responsibility for maintaining air quality and cleaning the air we pollute. And as trees and other plant life—the planet's natural systems for cleaning air—are destroyed, the problem becomes even more acute. The World Wildlife Fund estimates that an area of forest the size of Greece is lost each year, and

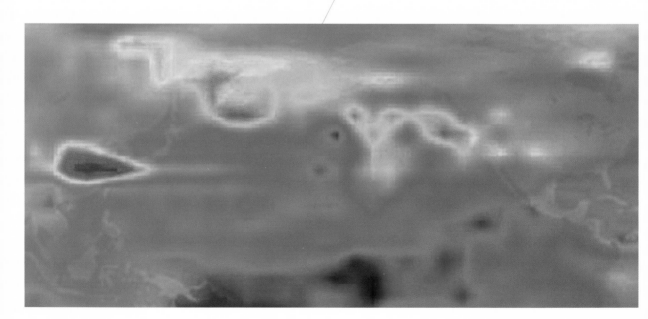

although sustainable timber supplies are available, most of this timber is never replanted.[1]

The City as Kidney

Cities are complex systems of inputs and outputs. As Herbert Girardet explains in his book *Creating Sustainable Cities,* "Cities, like other assemblies of organisms, have a definable metabolism, consisting of flow of resources and products through the urban system for the benefit of urban populations."[2] Once processed by the urban system, these resources form outputs such as airborne emissions, sewage, and industrial and household waste. Cities are responsible for a vast amount of waste, approximately 70 percent of which is typically returned, untreated, to the biosphere. The metabolism of our cities is a linear process that has little regard for the destination of waste products. The resulting quantity of emissions puts enormous strain on the natural processes in place to deal with them. We now face a situation where the outputs from our species as a whole far exceed the capabilities of our planet's treatment systems.

An analysis of our global carbon emissions reveals that between 40 and 50 percent are generated by buildings, 25 percent are from transport, and 25 percent come from industrial sources. This places a heavy responsibility on the shoulders of the construction industry. Designers need to address not only the issue of providing clean air for the occupants of buildings, but also the problem of making sure buildings don't pollute their surrounding environments. This challenge is key to the development of a sustainable future.

Rather than exhibiting the attributes of lungs—which merely consume oxygen—our cities should behave as kidneys, cleaning everything that passes through them and generating clean energy. This radical shift in attitude would create cities with a circular metabolism—cities that are able to effectively treat waste products and generate energy as well as consume it. In order to achieve this goal, architects, designers, and engineers need to embrace a combination of new technology and inherited architectural vernacular.

The Evolution of the Building Envelope

Early architecture existed to create comfortable internal conditions: Roofs, walls, floors, windows, and doors all evolved through time to fit the climate. This historical evolution has formed a vast lexicon of envelope typologies that designers can now draw upon.

In arctic environments, the Eskimo developed a unique strategy for retaining heat using very limited natural resources. The semi-spherical nature of their structures maximized floor area in relation to materials. Once built, the snow construction was completely

OPPOSITE **image of pollution levels over surface of the Earth**

1. "World Wildlife Fund Annual Report 2001," http://www. worldwildlife.org/ defaultsection.cfm?sectionid=152&new spaperid=15&contentid=425.

2. Herbert Girardet, *Creating Sustainable Cities* (Devon: Green Books for the Schumacher Society, 1999), 32.

sealed and then transformed into ice by repeated melting from the inside; the snow blocks quickly congealed into ice in the cold air. Hot air from the stove and the bodies inside the structure rose and was trapped inside the dome, which continued to melt and freeze over, forming a smooth, airtight ice surface. When the igloo was completed, a low wall of snow blocks was built around the outside to create an air space, which was filled with loose snow. The double wall and the snow insulation maintained the interior warmth.

On the other end of the spectrum, the humid climate of Malaysia averages air temperatures of between 73°F and 90°F. The traditional Malaysian house is designed to encourage ventilation by means of a number of devices: The building is raised on stilts to catch the strongest winds, and cool air from the shady ground space under the house is drawn up through the floorboards into the rooms above. The elongated structure with minimal partitions allows easy passage of air and cross-ventilation. Windy days are uncommon, but to make the most of the occasional winds the roof forms a wind-trap and distribution system. Vents are built into the top of the external walls to allow hot air to be drawn into the roof space, where it is then vented out. Air circulation through roof joints ensures effective ventilation of the roof and dissipates heat gain.

In the wide-ranging temperatures of the Middle East, low-energy ventilation systems have been part of building design for hundreds of years. Summer temperatures in Iran may range from 89°F to 120°F at midday, but fall to 68°F or less at night, and in the winter temperatures range between 68°F and 95°F, dropping down to 48°F at night. These extreme changes are reflected in the way buildings are designed and used. The badgir, or "wind catcher," was developed in Iran and other countries of the Persian Gulf. A fixed device capable of acting as a wind scoop and exhaust, it is open at the top on two or four sides, with a pair of partitions placed diagonally across each length. The wind towers are nine by nine feet and up to 21 feet high, with the upper section open to the wind in four directions. The badgir is able to catch breezes from any direction and channel cool air into the room. It also acts as a chimney. When the winds are low, the towers continue to ventilate the rooms.

In the closely packed houses of Hyderabad in Pakistan, wind scoops, which catch the wind at the area of greatest pressure and direct it into the building, have been in existence for at least 500 years. The greater their height above the roof, the more effective they are because of increased wind speed and reduced building interference. Wind scoops can also be placed in the ground some distance away from the building, and the supply air can be brought in through earth tubes. Though these ingenious cooling devices

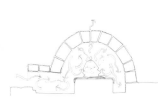

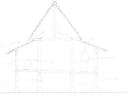

are strikingly different in appearance from those found in Iran, they are an equally appropriate solution to the environmental problems faced by this region.

In the temperate climate of the United Kingdom, the Georgian town house was an important development in the design of residential environments. Constructed from materials with good insulation properties and thermal mass credentials, these buildings maintain a relatively constant internal temperature. The Georgian sash window is a very effective way of introducing natural ventilation: The vertical sashes exploit the differences in air buoyancy and wind-generated air movement to allow variable control of ventilation.

Early skyscrapers such as the Home Insurance Building in Chicago created a new set of challenges for engineers. In these buildings, the plan was dictated by the need to accommodate ventilation systems, daylight, and a large number of occupants. While some of the early skyscrapers contained low-energy ventilation systems, the introduction of floor-by-floor air-conditioning systems created the kind of controlled environment hitherto never experienced in offices, and led to the gradual acceptance of this technology as the standard.

OPPOSITE FROM LEFT **igloo, Malaysian house, badgir, and wind catcher, with air-circulation diagrams**
LEFT **Georgian town houses**

LEFT **Home Insurance Building, Chicago**

The Impact of Air-Conditioning

Air-conditioning, or "manufactured air," as it was first described, was originally conceived as a way to control humidity. It wasn't until the beginning of the twentieth century that the term "air-conditioning" was used by a mill owner who combined moisture with ventilation, which actually conditioned and changed the air, thus controlling the humidity so critical in the textile mills. One of the first examples of a building air-conditioned for personal comfort was recorded in 1902, when the New York Stock Exchange was equipped with a central cooling and heating system. This system harnessed technology from the textile mills and adapted it for commercial buildings.

It was Willis Carrier, however, who did the most to promote controlled air. In 1902, realizing that air could be dried by saturating it with chilled water to induce condensation, Carrier created the world's first air-conditioning machinery: Liquid ammonia was pumped through a set of evaporation coils, and warm air in the room heated the ammonia, which evaporated, absorbing heat and cooling the air until it reached its dew point. The droplets that formed on the coils drained away and a fan returned cooler, dryer air.[3]

Not surprisingly, factories were quick to embrace "controlled air" because it increased productivity, and office buildings and schools were close behind. Between 1911 and 1930, many movie theaters also adopted air-conditioning, providing moviegoers with a pleasant indoor environment—and an escape from their hot, humid neighborhoods.

Air-conditioning as we know it bloomed after World War II, when resources were no longer scarce. The market for personal comfort was growing, and the demand for air-conditioners began to outstrip supply. Mass-produced machines were marketed as improving personal health, helping people get a better night's sleep, and keeping the interiors of houses clean. Mechanical cooling also made it possible for architects to design closed spaces with more glass—and to build these glass-walled skyscrapers just about anywhere.

Modern air-conditioning systems are now used globally to control the temperature, moisture content, circulation, and purity of air. We live in air-conditioned homes, travel to our air-conditioned workplaces in air-conditioned cars, shop in air-conditioned stores and malls, and enjoy sports in air-conditioned arenas. We have year-round choices of fresh or preserved foods kept cool or frozen, and we benefit from advances in medical services made possible by air-conditioning.

Unfortunately, these conveniences come at a great cost to the environment. And beyond the environmental implications, the human cost of over-conditioned spaces is well documented. In

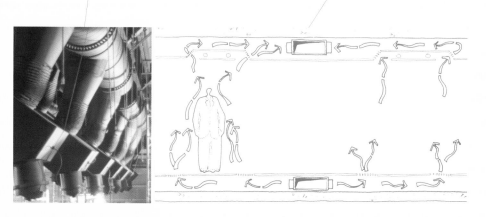

FAR LEFT **air-conditioning machine**
LEFT **diagram of air-conditioning system**

3. "Greatest Engineering Achievements of the Twentieth Century," National Academy of Engineering, http://www.greatachievements.org/greatachievements/ga_10_2.html.

cases of Sick Building syndrome, as it is commonly known, heavily air-conditioned spaces can actually significantly reduce comfort and productivity.

Post Air-Conditioned Architecture

The future of engineering environments lies in a new generation of buildings that use free energy to drive environmental systems, rather than functioning as hermetically sealed, artificial internal climates. By combining traditional wind-powered ventilation systems with new building management technologies, it is possible to design highly efficient buildings with extremely low emissions. These buildings not only have healthier environments—as they release less carbon dioxide into the atmosphere—they also cost less to operate than their air-conditioned counterparts.

The design of natural ventilation systems is now determined by a detailed analysis of the behavior of air within spaces. Computational Fluid Dynamics (CFD) analysis is a process of mathematically modeling the flow of air relative to temperature and pressure. Tools such as CFD and wind tunnel analysis allow engineers to form extremely realistic models of natural ventilation systems. This accuracy has led to the development of a number of different ways of driving natural ventilation systems.

One particularly successful device, the modern wind tower, was adapted from the vernacular architecture of the Middle East. When combined with modern technology, wind towers can be highly effective in powering ventilation systems. Wind towers were successfully used in the award-winning scheme for the Ionica Headquarters Building in the United Kingdom. Here, Battle McCarthy introduced an interactive facade, a central atrium with wind towers, ventilated hollow-core slabs with low-level air supply, and an integrated energy strategy with performance-monitoring systems. When they work together, these systems create comfortable office environments without the usual energy expenditure associated with air-conditioned spaces.

Ancient wind-scoop principles have also been used to create highly efficient wind-capturing devices capable of directing air down and through spaces with great effectiveness. The Bluewater shopping mall in Kent in the United Kingdom is one successful example: Battle McCarthy used wind scoops to ventilate the spaces naturally, supporting its central concept of the mall as a shopping avenue that possesses all the benefits of an outdoor street on a sunny day (sunshine, a fresh breeze, the sound of water, calming landscape, the aroma of spring flowers, and the enticing lure of freshly ground coffee), but filters out all of the unpleasant aspects of the street

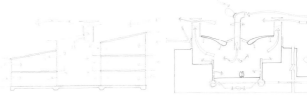

41

(cars, noise, pollution, crowded pavements, driving rain, and wind).

Wind towers can be augmented with solar energy to help drive ventilation systems. By maximizing solar gain in strategic locations within the extract system and the tower itself, solar energy can make the air rise faster, displacing air from below. This technique requires careful orientation of buildings to maximize solar penetration when needed and to allow for the control of excessive solar gain to avoid overheating.

The double skin is another ventilation device that makes use of solar energy. Research carried out by Battle McCarthy in association with Franklin Andrews on behalf of the United Kingdom Department of Environment, Transport, and Regions, has shown that double-skin buildings can reduce energy consumption and running costs by 65 percent, and can cut carbon dioxide emissions by 50 percent in the cold temperate climatic prevalent in the United Kingdom.[4]

Double skins can operate in many seasonal modes. In winter, the cavity acts as a thermal buffer zone between inside and out. This reduces space-heating requirements, as both conduction and infiltration gains are limited. Good solar penetration is achieved and acoustic protection is offered. This warm blanket of air around the building can be used to preheat the fresh supply air, saving energy expenditure and the emissions associated with it.

During mid-season, the skins can be opened, allowing natural ventilation. Fresh air is taken in without energy expenditure in heating or cooling, and blinds can be adjusted to let in or shut out light. Good daylight penetration is achieved and services can be relocated to the perimeter of the building, increasing net rentable space. Acoustic insulation is also reduced. During summer, the skin is sealed, and blinds within the cavity provide solar control. Space-cooling loads are reduced, increasing net rentable areas and reducing capital expenditure. Exhaust air is extracted through the cavity to remove heat gains.

One example of the use of this technique is the Commerzbank headquarters in Frankfurt by Foster and Partners. Here, a double skin was installed on each side of the triangular building. The double-facade cavity creates a sheltered zone with controlled infiltration, so the inner-skin, double-glazed tilt windows can be opened at all levels, despite external air pressure. The sky gardens, which occur every 10 stories, are ventilated at high levels, and oxygenated air is fed to the atriums to ventilate the internal atrium offices naturally. These two systems allow natural ventilation through both sides of the floor plate at all levels.

The Trombe wall, one of the earliest forms of double skin, was developed by the English horticulturist Edward Morse. Morse, who

RIGHT **view of Commerzbank Headquarters with air-circulation diagram** OPPOSITE LEFT **air-circulation diagram of Trombe wall** OPPOSITE RIGHT **diagram of labyrinth**

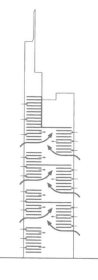

4. Battle McCarthy and Michael Wigginton with Franklin Andrews, "Environmental Second Skin Systems," scheduled for publication 2002.

observed that dark curtains drawn behind a window become warm and create warm air currents, built the first solar wall in 1881 (now known as the Trombe wall). Modern Trombe-wall techniques use high thermal mass concrete skins to maximize solar-energy absorption. The warm air currents inside the building can be used to assist natural ventilation, and the radiative heat from the thermal mass can be used for space heating.[5]

Another element frequently used in treating air is the Earth itself, which has a natural geothermal temperature that can be used to heat or cool air. Thermal labyrinths draw air through a complex of underground corridors to preheat or precool it. Typically constructed out of concrete to maximize thermal mass and notched to increase surface area, labyrinths can significantly reduce the energy requirements of buildings. The new National Museum of World Cultures in Gothenburg, Sweden, will use a thermal labyrinth to heat air during the winter and cool it during the summer. The air will be drawn down into the labyrinth through a remote wind scoop in an ecologically rich area.

Water can also be used to treat air in buildings. Introducing water features in and around buildings not only increases our sense of well-being and harmony, but can clean the air itself. (When air passes over water, its humidity rises, and microscopic droplets

cling to dust particles carried in the air. Their weight increases and they become too heavy for the air to carry—thus the air becomes cleaner.) In hotter climates, water can cool air as it evaporates. By directing air through the path of evaporating water, the air temperature is reduced significantly at the cost of a slight rise in humidity. This technique can be used to cool air in atrium and circulation spaces, where temperature is more important to comfort than lower humidity.

Air can be treated and conditioned, distributed and extracted in numerous ways that are both very low energy and produce zero emissions. But the story doesn't end there. We need to go further than simply reducing energy consumption and emissions. For some time, the environmental community has promoted the three R's: Reduce, Recycle, and Reuse. Recently it has been suggested that we add a fourth R: Recover. The remediation of environmental pollution and damaged natural resources is vital to the support of future sustainable development. We need to create a new kind of architecture that actively treats its waste products and cleans the air of our cities.

Architectural Eco-filters

A new generation of bioclimatic design has begun to address archi-

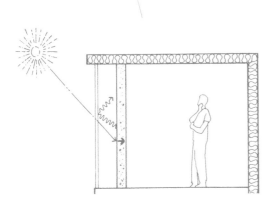

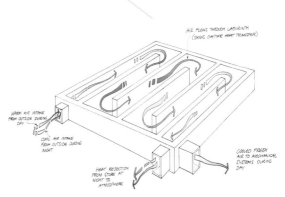

5. Trombe walls invented in 1881 (U.S. Patent No. 246,626) by Edward Morse of Salem, Massachusetts.

tecture's potential to clean the air. One of the leading practitioners of this school of design, Kenneth Yeang, has developed an intricate architectural language for expressing this philosophy. His solutions integrate not only air cleansing and recycling, but water conservation, recycling and reuse, on-site waste management systems, passive solar design, and on-site renewable energy generation.

These buildings could address the fourth R—Recover—by helping our natural resources remediate the environmental air pollution we have caused, as landscaping is now recognized as an effective way to manage emissions. Plants can scrub the air of pollutants and carbon dioxide, producing revitalizing oxygen. They can also improve internal environments by creating a more harmonious atmosphere. Along with the benefits of air treatment, deciduous climbing plants provide distinct seasonal advantages over metal sunshades. Dense foliage shelters the building from excessive solar gains during the summer, while the shedding of leaves in the winter allows direct solar heat gains. Plants also reduce noise pollution, acoustic reverberation, and, during the winter months, heat loss.

With this goal in mind, Battle McCarthy is currently working on a number of projects with Kenneth Yeang. Their master plan for Jabal Omar in the Al Haram valley near Mecca incorporates many bioclimatic features, including a linear green park that flows through the entire development on various levels. This not only creates a peaceful environment for the pilgrims using the development, it also introduces a vast ecological air filter into the scheme. The park is irrigated with recycled rainwater and conserved gray water from the development. The building spaces are cooled with ventilation towers that incorporate evaporative cooling, solar-driven stack-effect, and wind-tower extract systems. On a larger scale, the development acts as a wind harvester, a strategy that required careful analysis and modeling of building massing and orientation to maximize wind penetration at pedestrian levels and wind-tower locations.

Cities as Natural Power Stations

Bioclimatic cities could clean more carbon from the environment than they produce, which would redress the imbalance between the major carbon-producing areas of the world, such as North America, Europe, and Japan, and the areas where carbon production per capita is low, such as China and India. But in order to do that—and to create alternative energy strategies—we not only need to find new sources of energy to replace fossil fuels, but to develop new ways of thinking about energy generation. We should not see energy supply

LEFT **diagram of plants scrubbing the air**

OPPOSITE **environmental diagrams, Jabal Omar master plan, Al Haram valley, Saudia Arabia, T.R. Hamzah and Yeang**

as a linear process from fuel to power station to our cities—we should see our cities as power stations in themselves, self-sufficient in terms of electricity and heat, but also capable of supplying energy to surrounding towns.

The global carbon cycle is currently out of balance, increasing the likelihood of rapid global climate change. Atmospheric carbon dioxide levels are rising rapidly, and are now 25 percent above where they were before the Industrial Revolution; the Earth's atmosphere now contains some 200 gigatons more carbon than it did two centuries ago.[6] Some countries have agreed under the Kyoto Protocol to cut their emissions of greenhouse gasses by 5.2 percent below 1990 levels by 2010. The European Union has set itself a tougher target of a 12.5 percent reduction by the same deadline, while Britain is aiming for a 20 percent cut. By working toward these goals, we can secure the safety of what is fast becoming our most precious resource—our air. The path to this goal is difficult yet essential. As an Italian philosopher once said, "There is nothing more difficult to take in hand, more perilous to conduct, or more uncertain in its success than to take a lead in the introduction of a new order of things" (Niccolo Machiavelli, 1469–1527).

Guy Battle, cofounder of Battle McCarthy Consulting Engineers & Landscape Architects, is an internationally recognized leader in environmentally sensitive engineering and an instructor in environmental design at the Illinois Institute of Technology in Chicago.

The author wishes to acknowledge the contributions to this article made by Bob Thomas and Nick Foster.

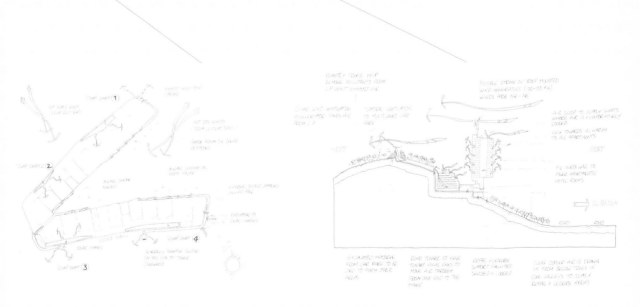

6. "Climate Change and Energy," World Resources Institute, http://www.igc.org/wri/climate/carboncy.html.

LIGHT & AIR

During the energy crisis in the 1970s, many architects proposed replacing the all-glass skins of skyscrapers and large-scale structures with smaller, sealed windows. This was supposed to reduce electricity use by keeping heat and air-conditioning from being lost to the exterior. Unfortunately, it resulted in buildings with poor indoor air quality that were overdependent on mechanical air-conditioning and artificial lighting. A few farsighted architects, however, designed large-scale buildings illuminated by the sun and naturally ventilated with double-skin windows that let in air but kept out noise and heat—a more logical approach when human comfort and health are taken into consideration. Now strategies for naturally ventilating and illuminating buildings are becoming more widely accepted. Architects are developing advanced techniques for providing natural air-conditioning in buildings of unprecedented size in the hottest of climates, as well as reviving older, forgotten strategies such as louvers and light shelves.

09.

PROJECT
Deutsche Messe AG Hannover Administration Building

For the 2000 Expo headquarters in Hannover, Germany, the architects developed a predominantly prefabricated structural system to minimize heavy construction at the site. It includes prefabricated columns, modular construction materials for the windows and vents, and precast concrete cladding. The building's most innovative feature is its double-skin ventilation system, which is driven by a ventilation tower that pulls air through the windows to cool or heat the office interiors.

ARCHITECT
Herzog + Partner
LOCATION
Hannover, Germany
YEAR:
2000

CLIENT
Deutsche Messe AG Hannover
STRUCTURAL ENGINEER
Sailer Stepan and Partner GmbH

MECHANICAL, ELECTRICAL & PLUMBING ENGINEER
Ingenieurburo Hausladen GmbH
GENERAL CONTRACTOR
BKSP Projektpartner GmbH

BUILDING TYPE
• high-rise
ENERGY GENERATION
• renewable energy use
• energy conservation systems
LIGHT & AIR
• daylight illumination
• natural ventilation systems
• monitored air quality
• operable windows

GREENERY, WATER & WASTE
• exterior gardens
• water conservation and reuse
CONSTRUCTION
• use of renewable materials
• use of local or regional materials
• modular construction techniques

URBANISM
• environmental planning
• public transportation access
• site reuse

Nord 1 Eingang Entrance

10.

Edificio Malecon

This 125,000-square-foot office building was designed for the planned commercial development zone of Puerto Madero, centrally located in Buenos Aires on the de la Plata River. The building's slim shape enhances natural ventilation, made possible by operable windows that take advantage of the cool breezes from the river. Direct summer sunlight is controlled with sunshades, and in the winter, when the sun is low, it illuminates the interior spaces. The structure was built on the foundations of an existing warehouse, reducing construction time, material waste, and landfill. Local, indigenous materials were used to reduce costs and, more important, the amount of transport required in the construction process.

ARCHITECT
Hellmuth, Obata + Kassabaum, Inc.

LOCATION
Buenos Aires, Argentina

YEAR
1999

CLIENT
Newside, S.A.

ENGINEER
Pablo Pschepiurca

CONTRACTOR
Constructura Sudamericana

BUILDING TYPE
- high-rise

ENERGY GENERATION
- renewable energy use
- energy conservation systems

LIGHT & AIR
- daylight illumination
- natural ventilation systems
- operable windows

GREENERY, WATER & WASTE
- water conservation and reuse
- exterior gardens

CONSTRUCTION
- use of local or regional materials
- modular construction techniques

URBANISM
- environmental planning
- public transportation access
- site reuse

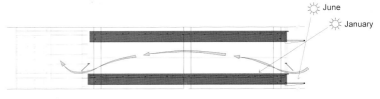

☀ June

☀ January

TOP **view of lobby**
ABOVE **ventilation and illumination diagram**

RIGHT **section detail of sunscreens and facade construction**

OPPOSITE **view of building**

A

B

RIGHT **view of facade showing sunscreens**

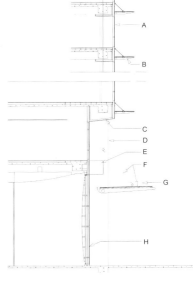

C
D
E
F
G

H

ABOVE **view of facade**

ABOVE **detail of double windows**

OPPOSITE **view of building showing service core**

RIGHT **axonometric diagram of double window with fish-mouth ventilator**

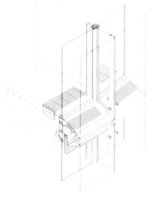

11. PROJECT
Highrise RWE AG

In this cylindrical office tower overlooking the city of Essen, the architects introduced a variety of environmentally sensitive technologies, including a "fish mouth" between each floor. Part air-intake and part sunshade, the fish mouths can be opened to ventilate the double-skin glass facade or closed to insulate the interior. The Building Management System, or BMS, controls temperature, light levels, and daylighting, allowing occupants to adjust the fish mouths and the blinds located between the double-skin glass. The building's energy is partially generated by photovoltaic panels on the roof-garden canopy.

ARCHITECT
Ingenhoven Overdiek und Partner

LOCATION
Essen, Germany

YEAR
1997

CLIENT
Hochtief AG

STRUCTURAL ENGINEER
Hochtief AG; Buro Happold Consulting Engineers

MECHANICAL ENGINEER
HL-Technik AG; IGK; Buro Happold Consulting Engineers

GENERAL CONTRACTOR
Hochtief AG

BUILDING TYPE
● high-rise

ENERGY GENERATION
● renewable energy use
● energy conservation systems

LIGHT & AIR
● daylight illumination
● natural ventilation systems
● monitored air quality
● operable windows

GREENERY, WATER & WASTE
● interior and exterior gardens

CONSTRUCTION
● modular construction techniques

URBANISM
● environmental planning

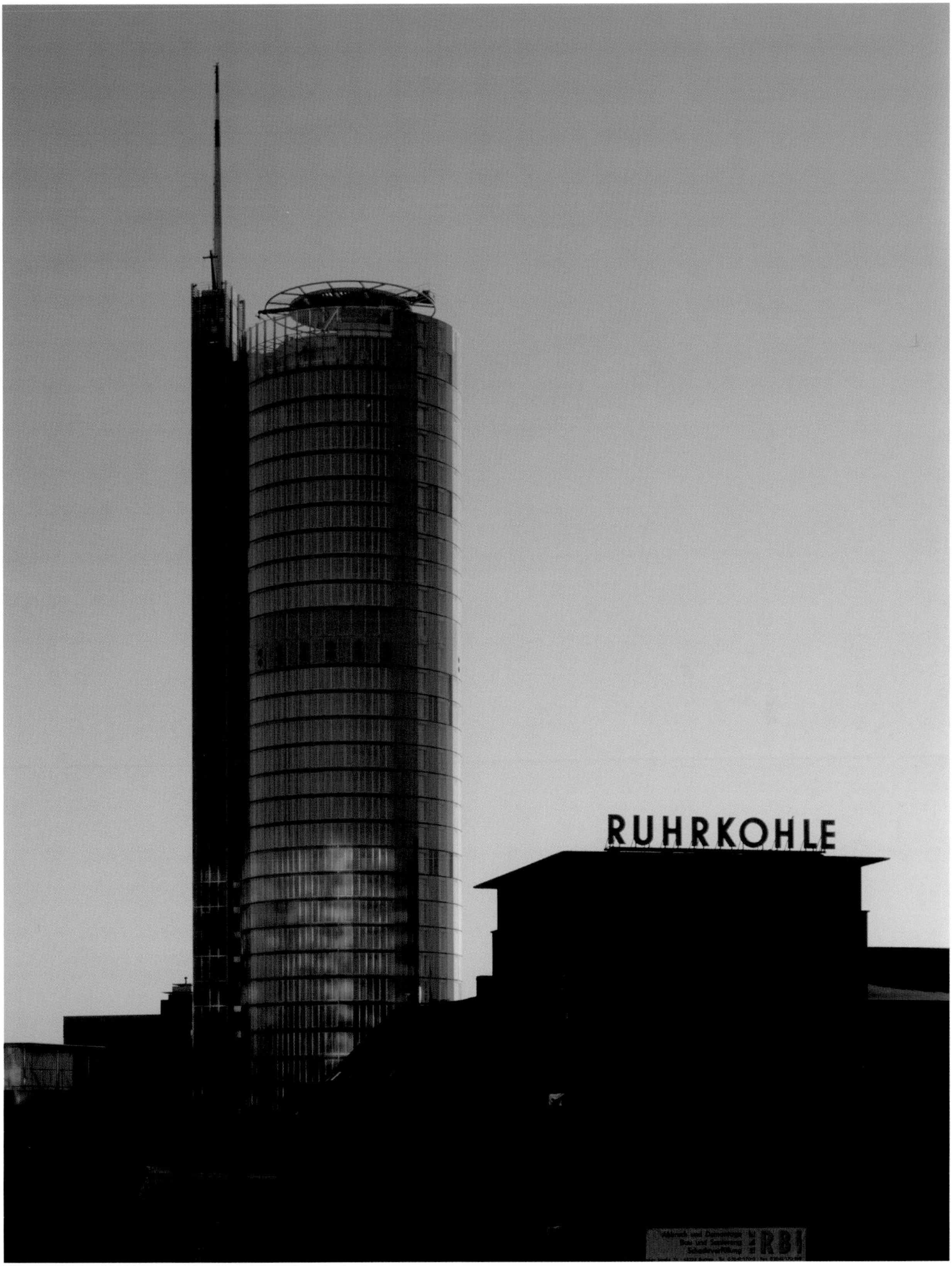
RUHRKOHLE

12.

The Tower Building
at Tower Oaks

Situated on a steep site adjacent to an interstate highway, the Tower Building was one of the first large-scale, environmentally sensitive office buildings in the Washington metropolitan area. The architects placed the building as close to the highway as possible to minimize its impact on the lushly wooded site. Natural daylighting was achieved with high-efficiency double-glazing that minimizes solar heat gain while allowing light to pass through to the interior. Acoustic controls in the exterior fenestration maintain a healthy sound level. The building's structural, interior, and exterior partitions were all designed using low-VOC, recycled, and recyclable products.

ARCHITECT
Kishimoto.Gordon P.C. Architecture

LOCATION
Rockville, Maryland

YEAR
2001

CLIENT
The Tower Companies

STRUCTURAL ENGINEER
SK&A

MECHANICAL ENGINEER
TOLK, Inc.

LANDSCAPE
EDAW, Inc.

CONTRACTOR
SIGAL Construction Corporation

BUILDING TYPE
- mid-rise

ENERGY GENERATION
- energy conservation systems

LIGHT & AIR
- daylight illumination
- monitored air quality

GREENERY, WATER & WASTE
- water conservation and reuse

CONSTRUCTION
- use of low-VOC materials

URBANISM
- environmental planning
- public transportation access

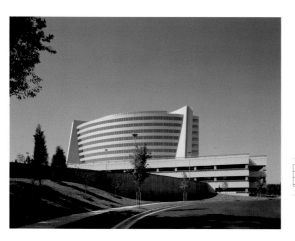

ABOVE **view of building from entry road**

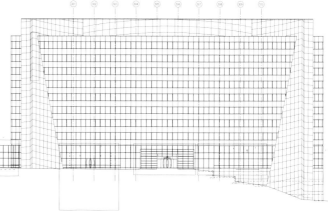

ABOVE **elevation**   BELOW **typical floor plan**   OPPOSITE **view of facade**

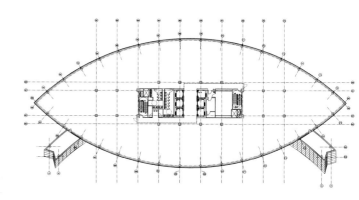

ARCHITECT
Kohn Pedersen Fox
Associates

LOCATION
Madrid, Spain

YEAR
1999–

CLIENT
Grupo ENDESA, S.A.

ASSOCIATE ARCHITECT
Rafael de la Hoz
Arquitectos SL

STRUCTURAL ENGINEER
Prointec

MECHANICAL, ELECTRICAL &
PLUMBING ENGINEER
Battle McCarthy
Consulting Engineers &
Landscape Architects

The new Endesa Headquarters Building, located in a developing business park in Madrid, was designed to satisfy the company's desire to consolidate its operations, project a global corporate image, and avail itself of the latest in low-energy technologies. Two bars of offices enclose a large atrium that functions as a public space and as an air-movement system for the building. Developed by Battle McCarthy Consulting Engineers, the air system provides natural cooling throughout the year. Air is drawn into underground tubes where it is cooled by the earth, and then the natural tendency of warm air in the atrium to rise (the "chimney effect") creates suction, pulling the cooler air out of the underground tubes and into the atrium and offices. To increase the escape of hot air and the velocity of incoming cooler air, large vents were placed on the roof. With this system, a high degree of comfortable indoor air-cooling is achieved without the use of mechanical air-conditioning.

BUILDING TYPE
● mid-rise

ENERGY GENERATION
● energy conservation systems
● renewable energy use

LIGHT & AIR
● daylight illumination
● natural ventilation systems
● operable windows

GREENERY, WATER & WASTE
● interior and exterior gardens

CONSTRUCTION
● modular construction techniques

URBANISM
● environmental planning

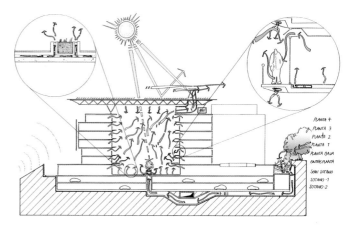

BELOW **photograph of model showing raised atrium roof with ventilators**

ABOVE **diagram of cooling and ventilation strategies**

OPPOSITE **model of atrium interior**

14

PROJECT
New Parliamentary Building

ARCHITECT
Michael Hopkins and
Partners

LOCATION
London, England

YEAR
2000

CLIENT
House of Commons,
Accommodation and
Works Committee

STRUCTURAL & BUILDING
SERVICES ENGINEER
ARUP Services Ltd.

PROJECT MANAGER
Schal International
Management Ltd.

CONSTRUCTION MANAGER
Laing Management Ltd.

COST CONSULTANT
Gardiner and Theobald

Michael Hopkins and Partners' design for the New Parliamentary Building features a ventilation system that is historically referential and provides an environmentally sensitive form of air-conditioning. A series of towers, which recall the site's Gothic architecture, draw air from ventilation ducts. The system uses the stack effect to pull cool air through vents in the lower floors and release hot air at the top. A central courtyard provides a public space and a focal point for the surrounding offices, which are naturally lit and were built using renewable materials. Most of the construction, both interior and exterior cladding, is modular. The building is connected to a new underground railway station, also designed by the architects, to encourage the use of mass transit.

BUILDING TYPE
- mid-rise

ENERGY GENERATION
- energy conservation systems

LIGHT & AIR
- daylight illumination
- natural ventilation systems
- monitored air quality
- operable windows

GREENERY, WATER & WASTE
- water conservation and reuse
- interior gardens

CONSTRUCTION
- use of renewable materials
- use of local or regional materials
- modular construction techniques

URBANISM
- public transportation access
- site reuse
- mixed-use building

LEFT **view of building showing ventilators on roof**

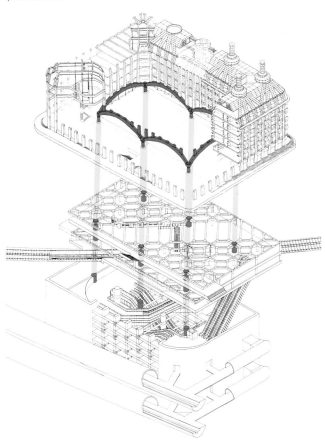

LEFT **interior courtyard with glass roof**

LEFT **photograph of office interior showing material and lighting concept**

ABOVE **exploded axonometric showing relationship of office and courtyard to transit station**

OPPOSITE **view of courtyard with greenery**

15

PROJECT
U.S. Federal Building

ARCHITECT
Morphosis Architects

LOCATION
San Francisco

YEAR
2001

CLIENT
General Services
Administration
(Region 9)

STRUCTURAL &
MECHANICAL ENGINEER
ARUP Services Ltd.

CONTRACTOR
Dick Corporation/Nibbi
Brothers, joint venture

The U.S. Federal Building consists of three distinct components: a thin tower that rises 18 stories along the northern edge of the site; a four-story annex projecting from the tower at the western edge of the site; and a large plaza that opens to the city. The southwest facade of the tower is clad in an undulating, perforated sunscreen installed over a full-height glass window-wall system. During the day, the sunscreen's panels can be opened and closed in response to the changing angles of the sun. The design evolved around three organizing concepts: the reduction of energy consumption through the integration of architectural and sustainable engineering principles; the creation of office environments that could influence the productivity and health of the working population with natural light and ventilation; and the redefinition of circulation and vertical movement paths in the building, using elevators, three-story sky lobbies, and compelling stairways to promote walking.

BUILDING TYPE
● high-rise

ENERGY GENERATION
● energy conservation systems

LIGHT & AIR
● daylight illumination
● natural ventilation systems
● operable windows

GREENERY, WATER & WASTE
● interior gardens

CONSTRUCTION
● modular construction
  techniques

URBANISM
● environmental planning
● public transportation access
● site reuse

RIGHT **transverse and
longitudinal sections
through building and site**

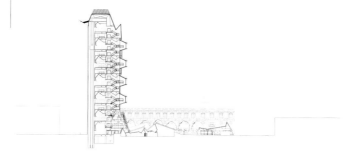

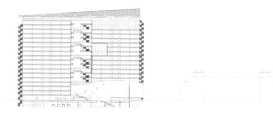

BELOW **diagrams of
naturally ventilated areas
and natural airflow in
offices**

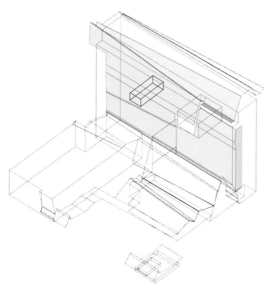

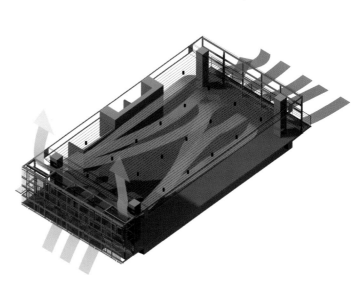

LEFT **view of sky gardens** ABOVE **computer rendering showing undulating curtain wall**

16. PROJECT
Eastgate

Working with ARUP Services Ltd., Pearce Partnership designed the largest commercial and retail project in Zimbabwe without air-conditioning. By studying termite mounds, the project team discovered a natural form of air-conditioning. During the day, the tops of the mounds are warmed by the sun, and at night the warm tops create suction, drawing cool air in at the base. Eastgate mimics this system: At night, cool air is draw in by the warm roof structure. The air chills the concrete slabs under the office floors and keeps the interior comfortable during the day. The sun is also used to light the offices and the central atrium.

ARCHITECT
Pearce Partnership

LOCATION
Harare, Zimbabwe

YEAR
1996

CLIENT
Old Mutual Properties

STRUCTURAL & MECHANICAL ENGINEER
ARUP Services Ltd.

CONTRACTOR
Costain Sisk Joint Venture

BUILDING TYPE
● mid-rise

ENERGY GENERATION
● renewable energy use
● energy conservation systems

LIGHT & AIR
● daylight illumination
● natural ventilation systems
● monitored air quality
● operable windows

GREENERY, WATER & WASTE
● exterior gardens
● water conservation and reuse

CONSTRUCTION
● use of renewable materials
● use of local or regional materials
● modular construction techniques

URBANISM
● environmental planning
● public transportation access
● mixed-use building
● site reuse

ABOVE LEFT **diagram of ventilation in termite mound**

TOP **view of building**
ABOVE **view of roofscape**

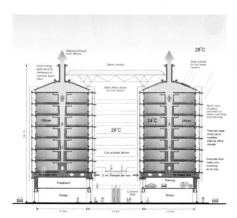

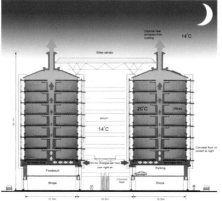

LEFT **diagrams of daytime and nighttime ventilation strategies**

ABOVE **view of courtyard**
RIGHT **view inside office with air intakes near ceiling**
FAR RIGHT **view of vegetated sunscreens**

Designed as the head office for one of the world's leading banks, the ABN-AMRO Bank World Headquarters provided an opportunity for PEI COBB FREED + PARTNERS to use its most recent research on curtain-wall technology. The facade incorporates ventilated cavity windows and automated blinds, and the building's heat-recovery system and light fixtures automatically adjust for changing light and occupancy levels, reducing energy consumption. The complex includes two office towers, a courtyard building with a dealing room for 600 dealers, an auditorium for 225, a congress hall for 400, and a 20-room meeting center.

ARCHITECT
PEI COBB FREED + PARTNERS Architects, L.L.P.

LOCATION
Amsterdam, Netherlands

YEAR
1999

CLIENT
ABN-AMRO Bank, NV

ASSOCIATE ARCHITECT
de Architekten Cie.

STRUCTURAL ENGINEER
Aronsohn Raadgevende Ingenieurs, BV

MECHANICAL ENGINEER
Technical Management, Amersfoort

CONTRACTOR
De Bank Combinatie

BUILDING TYPE
- high-rise

ENERGY GENERATION
- energy conservation systems

LIGHT & AIR
- daylight illumination
- natural ventilation systems
- operable windows

GREENERY, WATER & WASTE
- exterior gardens
- water conservation and reuse

CONSTRUCTION
- modular construction techniques

URBANISM
- public transportation access

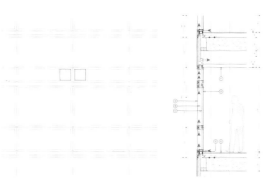

TOP **elevation**

ABOVE **plan, section, and elevation details of double-window systems**

ABOVE **view of building tower**

ABOVE **view of building showing various window types and landscape**

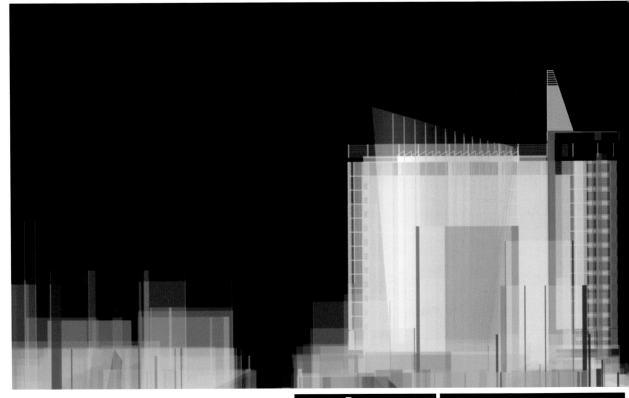

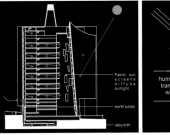

Fabric sun
screens
diffuse
sunlight

earth tubes

labyrinth

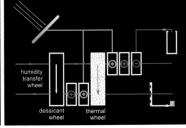

humidity
transfer
wheel

dessicant
wheel

thermal
wheel

18.

PROJECT
U.S. Courthouse

In their winning entry in a U.S. General Services Administration competition for a courthouse for the twenty-first century, Perkins & Will and Battle McCarthy Consulting Engineers reevaluated the courthouse building type according to environmental criteria. Adapting an architectural feature found in nineteenth-century public buildings, the project team developed a thermal cupola to drive a progressive cooling and heating strategy for the Los Angeles courthouse. In concert with a large, south-facing, curtain-wall solar collector, the cupola draws hot air out of the building to the roof, where it is collected to heat water. As in other natural cooling systems, air is drawn in at the base of the building to cool the offices and courtrooms at night. Blinds in the atrium shield the interior offices from the sun, and the building has a water-collection system and a process for naturally dehumidifying air through desiccants such as silicon.

ARCHITECT
Ralph Johnson with
Perkins & Will

LOCATION
Los Angeles

YEAR
2001–

CLIENT
U.S. General Services
Administration

STRUCTURAL ENGINEER
John A. Martin &
Associates, Inc.

MECHANICAL ENGINEER
Battle McCarthy
Consulting Engineers &
Landscape Architects

BUILDING TYPE
● high-rise

ENERGY GENERATION
● renewable energy use
● energy conservation systems

LIGHT & AIR
● daylight illumination
● natural ventilation systems

GREENERY, WATER & WASTE
● water conservation and reuse

URBANISM
● site reuse
● public transportation access

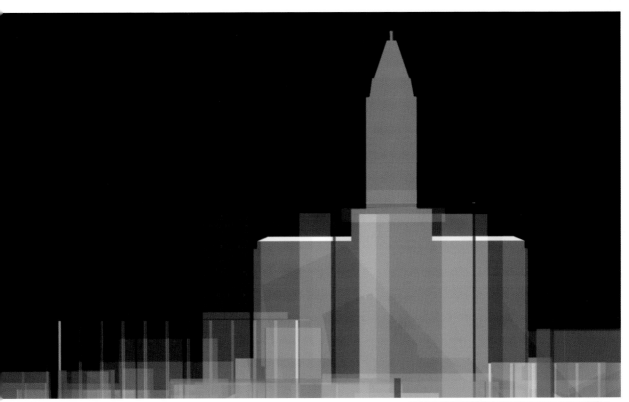

OPPOSITE **diagrams of passive ventilation and cooling strategies**

ABOVE **computer-rendered site elevation**

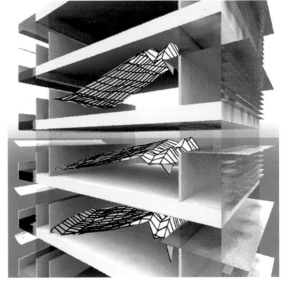

LEFT **entry elevation and section**

ABOVE **courtroom ventilation strategy**

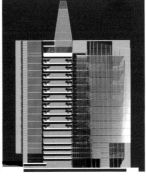

19.

PROJECT
David L. Lawrence Convention Center

ARCHITECT
Rafael Viñoly Architects

LOCATION
Pittsburgh

YEAR
2000–2003

CLIENT
Sports and Exhibition
Authority, Pittsburgh

STRUCTURAL ENGINEER
Dewhurst Macfarlane and
Partners, Inc.

MECHANICAL ENGINEER
Burt Hill Kosar
Rittelmann Associates

CONSTRUCTION MANAGER
Turner, P.J. Dick,
ATS Joint Venture

Located on one of Pittsburgh's rivers, the David L. Lawrence Convention Center is one of the first environmentally sensitive convention centers in the United States. The shape of the roof encourages natural cross-ventilation, taking advantage of the convection currents to draw fresh air from the river, and skylights provide natural light. The exhibition hall uses a low-temperature air-supply system that reduces the volume of air to be delivered, minimizing ductwork and energy consumption. Displacement ventilation is used throughout the facility to minimize the volume of air to be cooled.

BUILDING TYPE
- long-span

ENERGY GENERATION
- renewable energy use
- energy conservation systems

LIGHT & AIR
- daylight illumination
- natural ventilation systems

GREENERY, WATER & WASTE
- water conservation and reuse

CONSTRUCTION
- modular construction techniques

URBANISM
- environmental planning
- public transportation access
- site reuse

ABOVE **computer-rendered site collage**

BELOW **diagram of environmental strategies**

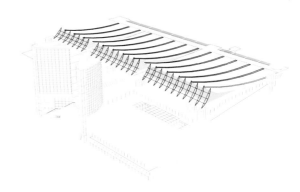

ABOVE **axonometric diagram of structural system**

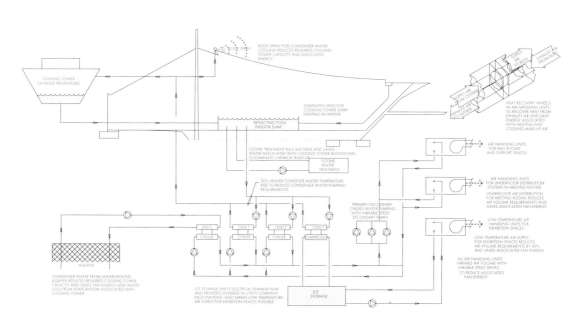

ABOVE **view of building from bay**

TOP **office interior**

ABOVE **corridor showing use of daylight illumination**

OPPOSITE **atrium with view of bay**

20.

PROJECT
Gap Inc. Offices

When the 1917 zoning codes were developed in New York City, they radically changed the massive, block-like shape of office buildings, transforming dark streets and office interiors into well-illuminated and ventilated spaces. In its design for Gap Inc.'s corporate offices, Robert A.M. Stern Architects, no stranger to historic precedent, references the forms of both the New York skyscrapers and the industrial buildings in the local San Francisco waterfront area. Punched with enormous windows, the building's stepped form works in concert with the large, skylighted atrium to provide generous amounts of natural light to the interior offices. Many of the corridors are also illuminated with daylighting, making what is typically the darkest of spaces pleasant. Raised floors conceal localized ventilation equipment, and recycled and renewable materials are used throughout the building.

ARCHITECT
Robert A.M. Stern Architects

LOCATION
San Francisco

YEAR
2001

CLIENT
Gap, Inc.

ASSOCIATE ARCHITECT
Gensler

STRUCTURAL ENGINEER
Middlebrook & Louie

MECHANICAL ENGINEER
C&B Consulting Engineers

ENVIRONMENTAL CONSULTANT
William McDonough + Partners, Dames & Moore

CONTRACTOR
Swinerton & Walberg

BUILDING TYPE
• high-rise

ENERGY GENERATION
• energy conservation systems

LIGHT & AIR
• daylight illumination
• natural ventilation systems
• monitored air quality
• operable windows

GREENERY, WATER & WASTE
• water conservation and reuse

URBANISM
• public transportation access
• site reuse

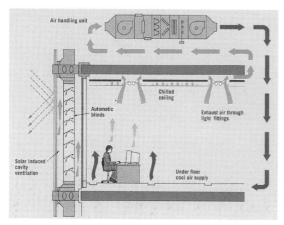

Air handling unit

Chilled ceiling

Automatic blinds

Exhaust air through light fittings

Solar induced cavity ventilation

Under floor cool air supply

ABOVE **ventilation, heating, and cooling strategy**

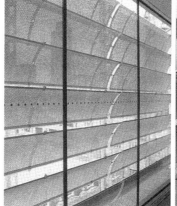

ABOVE **double window with blinds partially closed and open**

BELOW **elevation**

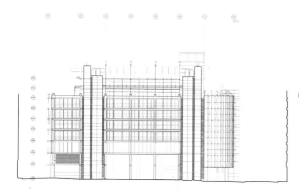

RIGHT **section detail of double window**

OPPOSITE **view of project**

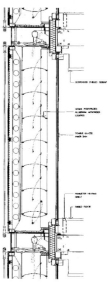

21. | PROJECT
Helicon

Operable windows are one of the easiest ways to reduce energy consumption, but noise and pollution can make them unpleasant to use. The architects and engineers of Helicon, however, found a way to naturally ventilate the interior of the building while ensuring that sound and dust pollution were kept to a minimum. The key to the solution: the ventilated double window. The heat that builds up behind the windows rises up and away from the office. On a hot day, this heat buildup is removed, and on a cold day the system uses it as a barrier between the interior and exterior. When removed, it can be reclaimed for heating water or the building's interior. Blinds within the ventilated cavity shield the interior from the sun. Unlike traditional window blinds, which are hung inside a room and give off heat, taxing the air system, the Helicon's blinds allow heat buildup to be removed from the exterior. The building also features a chilled ceiling, which provides additional low-energy cooling.

ARCHITECT
Sheppard Robson

LOCATION
London, England

YEAR
1996

CLIENT
London and Manchester Insurance

STRUCTURAL ENGINEER
John Savage and Associates

MECHANICAL ENGINEER
ARUP Services Ltd.

CONTRACTOR
Astec Projects Ltd.

BUILDING TYPE
• mid-rise

ENERGY GENERATION
• energy conservation systems

LIGHT & AIR
• daylight illumination
• natural ventilation systems
• operable windows

GREENERY, WATER & WASTE
• water conservation and reuse

CONSTRUCTION
• modular construction techniques

URBANISM
• public transportation access
• mixed-use building
• site reuse

22.

Manulife Financial

The U.S. headquarters for Manulife Financial is a 14-story building located in Boston's new commonwealth flats redevelopment area, adjacent to the convention center and world trade center. Wrapped in a nine-inch ventilated cavity curtain wall, it will be one of the largest examples of this technology in the United States. The base of the building was constructed with recycled materials, and on the roof is a garden of wild grasses and flowers. The project reflects Skidmore, Owings & Merrill's interest in curtain wall construction and environmental issues, evident in what some believe is the first use of the ventilated cavity in the United States, the 1978 Warren Petroleum Executive Headquarters in Tulsa, Oklahoma.

ARCHITECT
Skidmore, Owings & Merrill, L.L.P.

LOCATION
Boston

YEAR
2001–2003

CLIENT
Manulife Financial

STRUCTURAL, MECHANICAL, ELECTRICAL & PLUMBING/FP ENGINEER
Skidmore, Owings & Merrill, Chicago

CONTRACTOR
Clark/Suffolk

BUILDING TYPE
- high-rise

ENERGY GENERATION
- energy conservation systems

LIGHT & AIR
- daylight illumination
- natural ventilation systems
- operable windows

GREENERY, WATER & WASTE
- exterior gardens

CONSTRUCTION
- modular construction techniques
- use of renewable materials

URBANISM
- environmental planning
- public transportation access
- site reuse

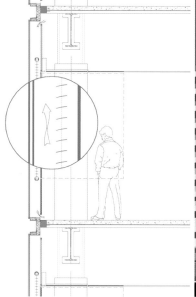

TOP LEFT **double-window facade system**
TOP RIGHT **model showing facade concept**
NEAR RIGHT **detail of double-window facade**
FAR RIGHT AND OPPOSITE **computer renderings of facade**

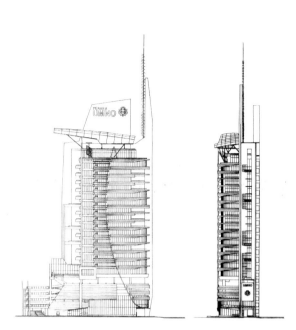

ABOVE **longitudinal and transverse elevations**

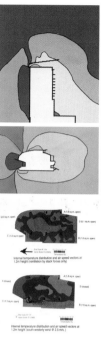

ABOVE **computer-generated airflow diagrams**

ABOVE **wing wall at back of building**

OPPOSITE **sunscreens and wing wall at side of building**

23. | PROJECT
Menara UMNO

In order to cool this 21-story office tower in the hot and humid climate of Malaysia using natural ventilation, all desks were located within 20 feet of an operable window, and "wing walls" were designed to draw outside air in. Other high-rises may have operable windows that provide fresh air, but a mechanical system is usually needed to remove the entire volume of interior air and bring in new air. T.R. Hamzah and Yeang designed this building so that air would be continuously replaced by the force of wind alone. In addition to creating a sense of connection to the natural environment, the architects were able to reduce the building's energy use by half.

ARCHITECT
T.R. Hamzah and Yeang, Sdn. Bhd.

LOCATION
Penang, Malaysia

YEAR
1998

CLIENT
South East Asia Development Corporation

STRUCTURAL ENGINEER
Tahir Wong, Sdn. Bhd.

MECHANICAL ENGINEER
Ranhill Bersekutu

VENTILATION CONSULTANT
Phil Jones

CONTRACTOR
Golden Amber Construction, Sdn. Bhd., JDC Corporation, Sdn. Bhd.

BUILDING TYPE
● high-rise

ENERGY GENERATION
● energy conservation systems

LIGHT & AIR
● daylight illumination
● natural ventilation systems
● operable windows

URBANISM
● environmental planning
● public transportation access
● site reuse

Vertiscapes:
The Skyscraper as Garden
by James Wines

It's an excellent time for the National Building Museum to be examining the future of the skyscraper. Since the September 11 destruction of the World Trade Center, the negative symbolic content of our nation's most identifiable building type has become the subject of unprecedented scrutiny in the popular, political, and design media. To make matters worse, urban developers are reeling from the economic implications of thousands of occupants moving out of mega-towers and seeking the perceived security of low-rise buildings and the protective sanctuary of suburbia. Additional threats to the skyscraper tradition are also being imposed by the burgeoning growth of the home-office media center. Computers now provide the convenience of reliable communication with corporate headquarters anywhere in the world and the luxurious advantage, for information-based employees, of living in sylvan surroundings, with only occasional trips to the city for office conferences, dining, and entertainment. As commuter traffic becomes increasingly unbearable, the statistical consequence of more than ten thousand American business executives converting to this digitally-connected suburban lifestyle every year seems destined to negatively affect the future of high-rise construction. And, of course, the development industry is now faced with the discomforting reality that terrorists view such structures as symbolic targets, which is certain to adversely affect developers' desire for trophy buildings. Recent

**Hanging Gardens
of Babylon**

reports from the real estate world reflect tenant fears and indicate that skyscrapers like the Empire State Building, the Transamerica Tower, the Sears Tower, and the AT&T Building have faced declining rental revenues—in some cases up to 40 percent—as city dwellers seek less ostentatious surroundings and increasingly favor structures under 20 stories. All of these deficits notwithstanding, the building industries in most major cities voice confidence in the future of the skyscraper and continue to showcase plans for ever taller buildings in New York, London, Hong Kong, Singapore, Kuala Lumpur, and elsewhere.

Given terrorists' perception that building height can be equated with capitalist exploitation and depraved Western values, however, this is probably the right moment to reassess the whole subject of verticality in architecture and its symbolic content. In this context, the shift of emphasis to Earth-centric concerns and the ecologically oriented theme of the National Building Museum's "Big & Green" exhibition and its accompanying book seem timely and prudent. If tall structures can represent something other than financial muscle, there is hope that they may ultimately communicate positive social and environmental values, as opposed to being seen as a perilous choice of habitat or as sitting ducks in a holy war.

With its emphasis on sustainable solutions for multistory buildings, this exhibition represents an effort to reconcile the profligate waste associated with the skyscraper with the need to meet new challenges of environmental stewardship. As the result of a generally indifferent attitude toward the environmental initiative by the architectural mainstream—further exacerbated by the reproachful and defensive posturing of certain green architects—ecological design has been bogged down by divisive politics and narrow definitions. It's time to view environmentalism as a much more inclusive opportunity for architectural innovation. But unless nature is seen as a motivational force for genuine philosophical change and a source of inspiration for design ideas, the green movement will continue to be regarded as marginal.

In the ancient world—before buildings were defined by real estate values—verticality mostly served as a symbolic bridge between the earthbound and the cosmological, or as a metaphorical representation of trees, plants, and the state of fertility. While tall structures were often fused with natural settings, the incorporation of vegetation into the actual fabric of architecture—as, for example, in the Gardens of Babylon—was a rare phenomenon. Monuments like Stonehenge and the dolmens of Neolithic societies, with their still debatable ceremonial functions, appear to be a combination of astronomical observatories and celebrations of the cosmic forces

Poulnabrone Dolmen, County Clare, Ireland, 2500 BC

that control the processes of nature. In early agricultural societies, this acceptance of a total dependency on the Earth's favorable blessings was manifested in a pantheistic belief that sun, rain, climate, and bodies of water required monuments to please multiple gods. In aboriginal cultures, as well, the presence of vertical totems signified a faith in animism and the capacity of the human body to exist in total harmony with nature. (Needless to say, most tall structures in today's urban centers represent the polar opposite of this respect for the environment and, in fact, invariably seem to be built in blatant defiance of the integrated systems of ecology.)

The drive to conquer nature coincided with the development of increasingly ambitious economic structures in early civilizations. Later on, the replacement of pantheism with the concept of a single, supreme God conveniently reflected the image and interests of man. It was also predicated on the notion that nature exists for man's convenience. There is every evidence that this ego-reinforcing theological premise became a turning point in the way in which Earth-centrism was interpreted in architecture, and that it set the stage for the use of verticality as a symbol of political, religious, and economic supremacy. For instance, in the early societies of the Middle East—Egypt, Sumeria, and Mesopotamia—the god-kings, in spite of their omnipotent relationship to indentured societies, still recognized that nature ruled their agricultural economies. Their

assortment of deities needed constant appeasement to assure fertility. These cultures' obelisks, columns, and towers usually featured a balanced mixture of iconographic references to animism, vegetation, and cosmology, as well as commemorating the heroic exploits of warriors and members of the royal family. In one example of the philosophical balance between nature and commerce in the ancient world, the Tower of Babel was built as a vertical consolidation of trade and enterprise, while the suspended Gardens of Babylon nearby venerated the landscape by releasing vegetation from its earthbound confinement.

By the Middle Ages, the notion of vertical thrust in architecture had become synonymous with civic and religious power. While Gothic cathedrals were usually encrusted with illustrative fragments drawn from nature, their celebratory imagery was consistently based on the idea of a supreme God (naturally, in the image of man) situated at the center of the universe. This trend dominated Western architecture throughout the late nineteenth and twentieth centuries. The impending homogenization of building design and the threatening onslaught of industrial technology was resisted by a few architects of the Art Nouveau (Guimard in Paris, Horta in Belgium, and Gaudi in Barcelona) whose architectural imagery incorporated the classic European urban scale and facade ornamentation of the nineteenth century, while embracing certain

**Tower of Babel, Pieter
Brueghel the Elder**

**Truro Cathedral, Cornwall,
England, 1880**

**Sagrada Familia Cathedral,
Barcelona, Antonio Gaudi,
1882–1926**

structural innovations of the Industrial Revolution. In the United States, Louis Sullivan's Carson, Pirie & Scott Department Store in Chicago and Bayard Building in New York demonstrated that new age functionalism could be brilliantly enhanced with forest glade—like sculptural embellishment. But as modernism gained momentum, these architects' richly floral motifs and sinuous evocations of nature's growing processes were regarded as evidence of a nostalgic attachment to the picturesque and irrelevant in the new world order. The advent of the Industrial Age—conspicuously manifested in Paxton's Crystal Palace in London and Eiffel's Tower in Paris—unleashed architecture's obsession with manufactured materials and new structural systems. With the exception of certain nature-based design interludes after the Paris Exposition of 1889—Art Nouveau, Arts and Crafts, the Jugendstil—architecture increasingly rejected the iconographic traditions connected with landscape, religious imagery, and handcrafted decoration. As the industrial dream became more vigorously identified with social reform, economic supremacy, and stylistic progressivism, glass-and-steel office towers and apartment blocks swept away most vestiges of landscape as a source of architectural symbolism and decorative embellishment.

By the 1920s and 1930s, modernism and constructivism had achieved global influence, and most contemporary designers continue to rely on these stylistic roots. In fact, there is very little indication that the natural environment influences today's architectural concepts, theories, and aesthetic choices. While contemporary green architecture is concerned with resource management and incorporates innovative environmental technology, it often relies on the aesthetic language of early modernism, revealing a continuing attachment to industrial materials and a preoccupation with the physicality of building construction. Many architects celebrate the virtuosity of how buildings are put together, as opposed to how well they respond to context and how sensitively they reflect ecological principles.

Frank Lloyd Wright remains a unique figure in twentieth-century architecture for his commitment to the fusion of structure and landscape long before ecology and sustainability were a part of conventional design discourse. His work is pivotal to any discussion of the iconic function of nature in the building arts. Describing his prairie high-rise building for the Price Corporation in Bartlesville, Oklahoma, he referred to the structure as "the tree that escaped the forest." Wright's poetic connection between the isolated tower—in this case, a visionary structure that combined living and office space—and its extraction from some distant woodland is an idea that seems fundamental to the "Big & Green" project. Wright prophesied that the building would "enable similar ones, though infinite in variety rising

Farmers and Merchants Union Bank, Columbus, Wisconsin, Louis H. Sullivan, 1919

Eiffel Tower, Paris, Gustave Eiffel, 1887–1889

drawing of Price Tower, Bartlesville, Oklahoma, Frank Lloyd Wright, 1956

as gleaming shafts of light, tall as you please from every village in the country." Viewed from the perspective of today's explosive urban populations and the inevitable growth of cities over the next decade, his concept carries other messages. It suggests that the relationship between nature and architecture can reflect a combination of geomorphic (territorial) and biomorphic (organic) sources. It also proposes that the future city and its clusters of tall buildings can be seen as kind of orchestrated forestation, where the mutable and evolutionary processes of nature are reflected in the philosophy of urban growth, choices of building imagery, greening of public spaces, and methods of achieving sustainability. Wright designed a second early building, the St. Mark's Tower of 1929, around a treelike core with balconies of cascading vegetation, a fusion of landscape and skyscraper that has also provided a significant precedent for some of the work in this exhibition.

Fearing a loss of stylistic identity and the sacrifice of formal commitments, most designers still cling tenaciously to the view that including vegetation in architecture would compromise the sculptural integrity of their work, would be perceived by colleagues as a submission to picturesque devices, and would represent a violation of those etched-in-granite principles of abstract art. Furthermore,

architects frequently view the field of landscape architecture as a marginal discipline, and its services are usually engaged after the building is complete and the client has requested a charm bracelet of lollipop trees around the "big event." These traditional prejudices are beginning to fade—especially in the face of scientific evidence that increased vegetation in cities is a major health imperative—but evidence of designers trying to reshape the basic content of architecture around the symbiotic relationships in nature is still very rare. This resistance to incorporating natural elements in buildings suggests a fundamental question: Just as factories, bridges, airplanes, and structural materials became inspirational sources for architects in the 1920s, why can't the wealth of ideas found in ecology, biochemistry, hydrology, geology, and botany give form to the future of tall buildings?

Many of the leading architects of the past century have been inspired by environmental sources, but the results have usually been resolved in terms of organic form that simulates various shapes found in nature. The majority of recent structures in this vein—from Richard Meier's Getty Center to Frank Gehry's Guggenheim Bilbao—have incorporated such references within the traditional confinement of a form- and space-making process (based on modernist, cubist, and constructivist traditions). This has resulted in a continuing legacy of objects sitting *in* the environment,

drawing of apartment, Price Tower

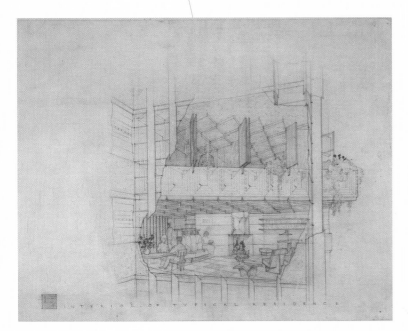

as opposed to a fusion of elements seen *as* the environment. There is a broad conceptual difference here, which indicates the need to fill some of the following gaps in current organic design thinking.

In most cases, recent examples of organic architecture do not favor a fusion of vegetation and structure—they lack an integrative interpretation of trees and plants in which natural elements are considered as much a part of the building design as steel, glass, and masonry. Another missing ingredient is a commitment to climate control and resource conservation, based on site-specific imperatives, prevalent weather conditions, and green design principles.

Third, as those ubiquitous people-free photographs in design magazines continue to attest, most architects are locked into a myopic notion of their work as a primarily visual statement. This attitude, in turn, leads to the media-driven fear that the sculptural qualities of a building might be blocked from view by an invasion of occupants. Design is an extension of the human body, but prosthetic considerations—both physical and psychological—are just beginning to become a priority.

During the past decade, the way people see the world has been increasingly shaped by computers, mass media, and an awareness that all is not well with the environment, influences that are far removed from the physical and political forces that shaped early modern design. The fourth missing element in organic design,

therefore, is a willingness to approach architecture in a way that reflects these influences and is consistent with the digital information revolution and the interactive characteristics of the natural world. The search for a persuasive imagery and meaningful content in architecture ought to reflect a philosophy of integrated systems, which might include a hybrid fusion of representation and abstraction, a questioning of the basic definitions of architecture, and a process of generating ideas from the widest possible range of contextual sources. If architects are really interested in producing relevant work, it is probably fruitless to rely on inspirational baggage identified with the Industrial Age.

In addition to Wright, architects who have addressed one or several of the challenges listed above include Le Corbusier, Moshe Safdie, Lucien Kroll, Roger Ferri, and Kenneth Yeang. Le Corbusier's Unité d'Habitation project of 1952 in Marseilles included a roof garden and multiple public spaces in the sky, confirming his dedication to social housing and his belief in people's right to experience abundant sunlight as an entitlement of Industrial Age living. His elevated garden became a microcosm of the surrounding landscape, like the Japanese concept of borrowed scenery. (Le Corbusier's approach to integrating structure with context was based on classical models and an admiration for the majestic siting of buildings at the Acropolis, as opposed to the idea of melting architecture into its

Unité d'Habitation, Marseilles, France, Le Corbusier, 1952

surroundings, but the Marseilles housing block was built before issues of environmental impact and sustainability were of concern, so neither this nor the extensive and ecologically questionable use of concrete can really be blamed on the architect.]

For the Expo '67 in Montreal, Moshe Safdie introduced a fragmented kit-of-parts structure called Habitat, which offered a revolutionary interpretation of clustered housing. Borrowing ideas from Mediterranean hill towns, he set the stage for a wide range of subsequent buildings that rejected symmetrical composition and the rigorous formalism of modern design. The stacked and casually skewed apartments provided a wide range of opportunities for inhabitants to plant balcony gardens, follow haphazard patterns from level to level, experience inside-outside living relationships, and participate in a unique social life not available in conventional apartment buildings. In architectural terms, Safdie's Habitat respected people's prosthetic needs by accommodating their unpredictable movements through space. Admirably, the aesthetic quality of the structure reflected an organic growth process instead of attempting to simulate the curvilinear shapes found in nature.

Similar, but much bolder in its freewheeling collage approach, the 1974 Medical Faculty Building at the University of Louvain by Belgian architect Lucien Kroll resembles a massive readymade by Marcel Duchamp. The core building block of this housing unit

is relatively conventional. Its visual drama derives from a facade encrusted with stylistically diverse and randomly overlapping windows, doors, and balconies that seem to have sprouted like vegetation on a mountainside. The seemingly arbitrary component parts have inspired inhabitants to add their own contributions over the years. These unrestrained additions have hyperbolized the image of spontaneous growth within the building, creating a true architecture of evolution and change.

In a brilliant moment of inspiration in 1976, the architect and interior designer Roger Ferri produced a visionary New York skyscraper enveloped from top to bottom by a band of forestation. In the terraced sections where vegetation invaded the building, the edges of the structure were fragmented, as if eaten away by the encroaching greenery. Ferri's intention was to expand on Wright's concept of the tree that escaped the forest by inserting an Arcadian tower of pines, waterfalls, and gorges in the center of Manhattan. In contrast to the St. Mark's Tower, which would have soared above adjacent town houses, Ferri proposed a living tree in a forest of remnants from the Industrial Age. Ferri, who died of AIDS in 1991 at the age of 42, pioneered the skyscraper as garden. His verdant tower forecasted the work of Emilio Ambasz and Kenneth Yeang, two architects who have become influential in the greening of the high-rise.

Emilio Ambasz uses topography and vegetation as narrative ele-

**Habitat, Montreal, Canada,
Moshe Safdie
and Associates, 1967**

**Medical Faculty Building,
University of Louvain,
Belgium, Lucien Kroll, 1974**

ments to create high-rise utopias, treating structure as minimal geometry that frames the landscape. His 1995 ACROS Building in Fukuoka, Japan, is a 15-story structure distinguished by a massive wall of vegetation that ascends the edifice in a stair-like configuration. People who visit the ziggurat or work in its offices use what they call the "growing facade" for strolling or sunbathing. Like Ferri, Ambasz sees the architect as a custodian of the environment as well as a communicator of the iconic relationships between structure and landscape. He believes that the true green city of the future will be a metropolis where designers are able to comfortably fuse elements considered to be "real nature" with those thought of as "man-made nature." As he observes, "Even those areas that appear to be wild forests and virgin landscapes are almost inevitably the product of human intervention at one time or another."

Kenneth Yeang's firm, T.R. Hamzah and Yeang, has built a global practice devoted to ecological design. Yeang's work is not only aesthetically imaginative, it also explores the scientific frontiers of green design and the social and contextual implications of vertical construction. His firm has developed an extraordinary database with information on climate control, meteorological factors, geology, biochemistry, botany, resource management, and a range of other factors that affect the future of architecture. His work is based on the idea that the natural environment consists of both abiotic and biotic constituents, which function in harmony to form ecosystems. Yeang believes that as societies become increasingly industrialized, more and more of the environment risks accumulating an imbalance of inorganic materials. Consequently, it becomes the role of architecture to reflect the model provided by nature and maintain a responsible equilibrium. Many of the skyscrapers designed by T.R. Hamzah and Yeang are based on integrative systems, and some are as elaborate in their incorporation of plants and trees as Roger Ferri's imaginative precedent. Yeang rightfully sees vegetation as an essential element that assures quality of life—the oft-repeated equation that one tree means four people can breathe—and he is convinced that every building should include an intrinsic weave of landscape and structure.

In 1980, my New York–based architecture firm, SITE, designed a project we called High-rise of Homes, which later became a traveling exhibition. The premise was relatively simple: We proposed an experimental high-rise housing project of 15 to 20 stories, to be located in a densely populated urban center. The building was intended for mixed-income families and included both shopping and residential facilities. The only obviously designed component was a steel-and-concrete matrix, which supported a vertical community of private houses clustered in village-like communities on each floor. Every level was treated as a flexible platform with divisions that

New York skyscraper, Roger Ferri, 1976

could be purchased as separate real estate parcels. A central elevator and mechanical core serviced the individual houses, gardens, and interior streets.

The concept was based on our observation that most twentieth-century, architect-designed, multistory buildings eliminated the opportunity for inhabitants to achieve any expression of individuality. The High-rise of Homes offered apartment dwellers the unique advantages of gardens and the freedom to create a highly personalized identity by choosing facade treatments and landscaping. Our intention was to shift the measure of aesthetic evaluation to include the risky element of chance—to create a tenant-activated collage that encouraged indeterminacy, idiosyncrasy, and cultural diversity. In this sense, the project became the equivalent of what Duchamp referred to as "canned chance."

Part of the controversy that surrounded the High-rise of Homes was caused by its presumed lack of seriousness and the proposition that the architect's contribution should be nothing more than a support matrix. In retrospect, this idea seems even more relevant, as it questions many of the basic premises of twentieth-century design and suggests a shift of emphasis from the sculptural to the conceptual. It allows urban dwellers to assert their identities in the cityscape, it animates the high-rise with spontaneous garden spaces, it allows evidence of cultural diversity, and it invites occupants to become part of a living iconography.

With the future of skyscrapers in question, the mission of environmental reform unfulfilled, and the messages of September 11 still incomprehensible, this exhibition may be an ideal catalyst for exploring these issues. In most respects, the World Trade Center embodied the polar opposite of the values being honored by the National Building Museum. From a tragic but highly instructive perspective, the Twin Towers have come to represent so much of what went wrong with twentieth-century architecture. This 1960s example of urban renewal and its subsequent demise graphically reinforce the urgent need for integrative green technology, a greater sensitivity to the value of incremental community growth, and a respect for urban dwellers' individual identities. The WTC's checklist of failures includes the elimination of a vibrant and historic lower Manhattan neighborhood to make way for omnivorous development, the erection of oppressive towers as an endorsement of financial supremacy, and the construction of a concrete wasteland in the name of public space. With a cavalier disregard for people's health, these skyscrapers demonstrated a preference for toxic-waste-producing building materials (especially aluminum and asbestos), the obscene consumption of natural resources for construction and maintenance, and a minimal commitment to air-cleansing vegetation in the surrounding environment.

**High-rise of Homes,
James Wines, 1982**

Furthermore, the Port Authority of New York and New Jersey, the building's owner, had to contend with disappointing rental revenues for more than 30 years until, finally, the towers' symbolic content provoked the vengeance of Islamic terrorists. This four-decade history suggests that the World Trade Center was a doubtful contribution to New York City from its inception. It also mandates that the skyscraper of tomorrow be rethought.

The twentieth century began with a flood of idealistic manifestos from architects extolling the virtues of new building technologies and their relation to social reform. Rarely did these prophetic designers foresee the negative effects of industrialization or the rampant growth of consumer culture. For the modernist pioneers, manufactured products were synonymous with liberty and unlimited opportunity. They never imagined the devastating consequences of these seductive artifacts: global warming, declining resources, shrinking water supplies, polluted rivers, an increased incidence of cancer, and overpopulation. A convincing manifesto for today would have to question everything the early theories and proclamations extolled.

"Big & Green" is about this questioning process. It advances architecture's most compelling dialogue by confronting the ominous environmental predictions for the coming decade. While many of the examples in the exhibition and the book focus on green technology as the key to avoiding these doomsday scenarios, a number of the works illustrate the parallel importance of contextual, iconographic, psychological, and aesthetic elements. They show us that when trees, plants, terrain, and ideas inspired by the science of ecology are used as sources of imagery, it expands not only the communicative power of the building arts, but their social relevance as well.

James Wines, the founder and president of SITE Projects, Inc., is a professor and former head of the department of architecture at Pennsylvania State University.

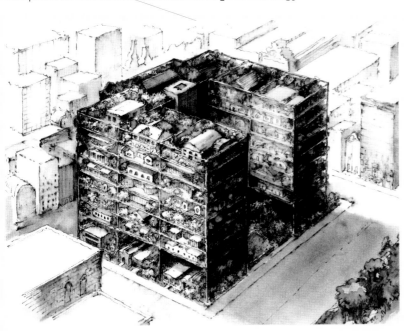

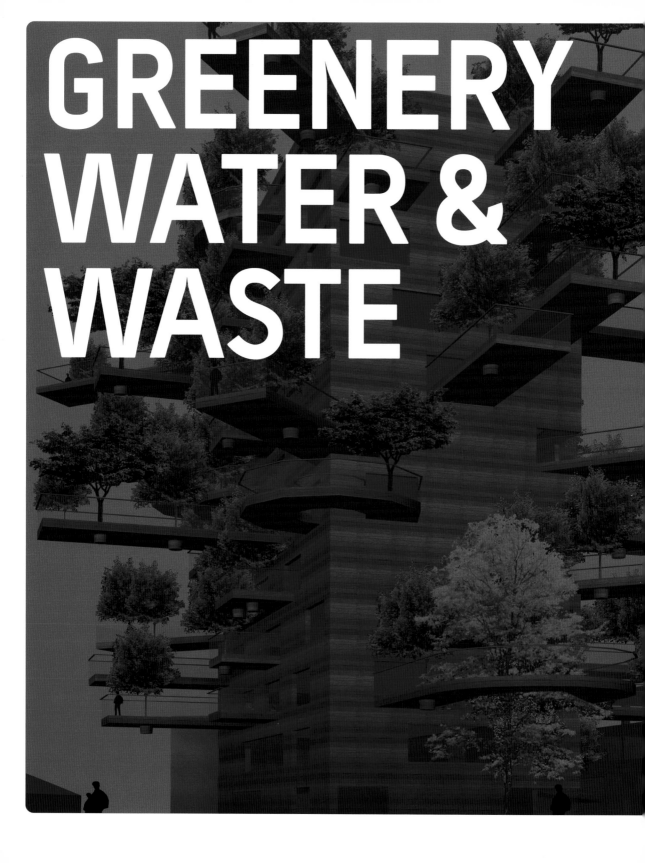

GREENERY WATER & WASTE

Understanding the relationship between greenery, water, and waste is important as architects attempt to curb water consumption, reduce wastewater, and use natural plant materials to mitigate the impact buildings have on their surroundings. Large buildings can consume millions of gallons of water a day, while during a single rainstorm millions of gallons can be lost to practical use, as water runs off into sewers or into ground water where it absorbs the toxins from construction materials. Engineers and architects are now collaborating to develop ways of using this run-off as undrinkable gray water in sinks and toilets. Greenery, which helps to promote health by converting carbon dioxide into oxygen, is also being incorporated into buildings to treat chemically saturated run-off water before it is released into the surrounding environment. In some instances, greenery and other living organisms are even being used to transform wastewater into drinking water.

Widely considered to be the world's first environmentally sensitive high-rise, the Commerzbank is also the tallest building in Europe. The green roof of Foster and Partners' influential 1977 Willis Faber and Dumas Headquarters is reinterpreted in the Commerzbank as staggered gardens, located every 10 floors. The building, which also features double-glass walls that naturally ventilate the offices, sets a new standard for the high-rise, eschewing the monotonous repetition of floors so common in most tall buildings.

ARCHITECT
Foster and Partners

LOCATION
Frankfurt, Germany

YEAR
1997

CLIENT
Commerzbank, Frankfurt

ENGINEER
ARUP Services Ltd.

CONTRACTOR
Hochtief AG

BUILDING TYPE
- high-rise

ENERGY GENERATION
- energy conservation systems

LIGHT & AIR
- daylight illumination
- natural ventilation systems
- monitored air quality
- operable windows

GREENERY, WATER & WASTE
- interior gardens
- water conservation and reuse

CONSTRUCTION
- modular construction techniques

URBANISM
- environmental planning
- public transportation access
- site reuse

RIGHT **view of courtyard from sky garden**

BELOW **typical floor plan showing offices and sky garden**

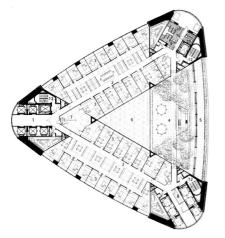

RIGHT **section showing sky gardens every six floors**

OPPOSITE **view of building**

This 41-story cylindrical tower, which will house the London-based staff of one of the world's leading reinsurance companies, includes offices, retail areas, and a public plaza. The building features a series of rotating, radiating floors linked by spiraling light wells that contain greenery to break down the scale of the building and create pressure differentials to improve natural ventilation. Fresh air is drawn in at each floor through slots in the cladding, and exhaust air is vented to the outside or recycled to provide heat to the building. The system is expected to be so effective that air-conditioning will not be required for most of the year, resulting in significantly less energy consumption than in conventional office buildings.

ARCHITECT
Foster and Partners

LOCATION
London, England

YEAR
1997–2004

CLIENT
Swiss Re

STRUCTURAL &
MECHANICAL ENGINEER
ARUP Services Ltd.

CONTRACTOR
Gardiner and Theobald

BUILDING TYPE
● high-rise

ENERGY GENERATION
● energy conservation systems

LIGHT & AIR
● daylight illumination
● natural ventilation systems
● monitored air quality
● operable windows

GREENERY, WATER & WASTE
● interior gardens
● water conservation and reuse

CONSTRUCTION
● modular construction techniques

URBANISM
● environmental planning
● public transportation access
● mixed-use building
● site reuse

ABOVE **sketch showing environmental concepts, Norman Foster**

OPPOSITE **photomontage of tower in City of London**

RIGHT **elevation showing diagonal structural system and section showing spiraling atriums**

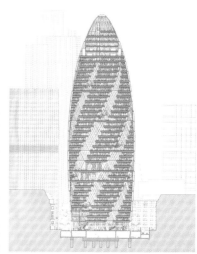

A radical marriage of mid-rise building and public park, MVRDV's Dutch Pavilion presents the visitor with a series of stacked landscapes based on natural and man-made environments in the Netherlands. Visitors pass through a polder, a forest, and a marsh, ending up on the roof, which has a lake and a viewing platform. A prototype for the introduction of nature in physically dense cities, the pavilion comes out of MVRDV's ongoing research into stacked ecosystems; it was first proposed as a stacked park in an unbuilt project and then as stacked pens for livestock (also unbuilt). The design for the Dutch Pavilion initially included a water-reclamation system to capture rainwater and distribute it throughout the building. As built, it runs on energy-generating windmills.

ARCHITECT
MVRDV

LOCATION
Hannover, Germany

YEAR
2000

CLIENT
Foundation Holland World Fairs, The Hague

STRUCTURAL ENGINEER
ABT Structural Engineers

MECHANICAL ENGINEER
TM, Amersfoort

CONTRACTOR
HBG/Wayss & Freitag

BUILDING TYPE
● mid-rise

ENERGY GENERATION
● renewable energy use
● energy conservation systems

LIGHT & AIR
● daylight illumination
● natural ventilation systems

GREENERY, WATER & WASTE
● interior gardens
● water conservation and reuse

URBANISM
● environmental planning
● public transportation access

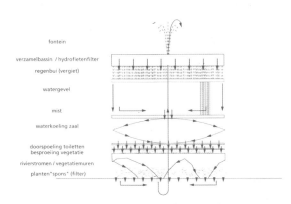

fontein

verzamelbassin / hydrofietenfilter

regenbui (vergiet)

watergevel

mist

waterkoeling zaal

doorspoeling toiletten
besproeiing vegetatie

rivierstromen / vegetatiemuren

planten "spons" (filter)

ABOVE **view of forest floor and diagram of water distribution**

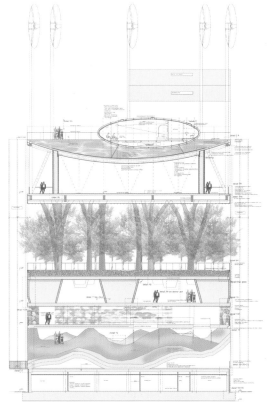

ABOVE **section showing stacked ecosystems**

OPPOSITE **view of building**

27. PROJECT
3D-Garden

Frank Lloyd Wright and Le Corbusier both compared their tall building designs to trees, and Wright went so far as to configure his St. Mark's Tower with a trunk-like central structure and branch-like cantilevered floors. In MVRDV's design for a multistory apartment house in the Netherlands, the apartment block similarly stands in for the tree trunk and balconies resemble branches. MVRDV reinforces this resemblance by proposing that trees be planted at the end of most of the balconies so that, eventually, the entire structure will be covered in greenery. A striking aesthetic statement, the trees will also help cool the building, filter the surrounding air, and control water run-off.

ARCHITECT
MVRDV

LOCATION
Hengelo, Netherlands

YEAR
2001–

CLIENT
Assen Projekten BV

STRUCTURAL ENGINEER
Pieters Bouwtechniek

TREE ENGINEER
Bomencentrum
Nederland

BUILDING TYPE
- high-rise

LIGHT & AIR
- daylight illumination
- natural ventilation systems
- operable windows

GREENERY, WATER & WASTE
- exterior gardens
- water conservation and reuse

URBANISM
- environmental planning
- public transportation access
- mixed-use building
- site reuse

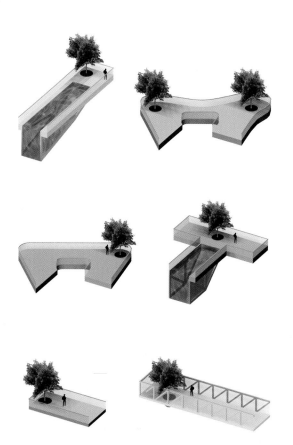

ABOVE **computer rendering of balconies with gardens and pools**

ABOVE **section showing relationship between balconies and apartments**

OPPOSITE **computer rendering**

PROJECT
British Pavilion, Expo '92

ARCHITECT
Nicholas Grimshaw
and Partners

LOCATION
Seville, Spain

YEAR
1992

CLIENT
Department of Trade and
Industry

STRUCTURAL & MECHANICAL
ENGINEER
ARUP Services Ltd.

WATER-FEATURE CONSULTANT
William Pye Partnership

CONTRACTOR
Trafalgar House
Construction
Management Ltd.

The British Pavilion was a temporary structure built for the Expo in 1992, but it remains one of the world's most innovative climatically responsive long-span spaces. Nicholas Grimshaw and Partners dealt with the challenge of reducing the heat generated by audiovisual equipment, large gatherings of people, and the hot climate of Seville with a combination of louvered shades and natural, water-driven cooling systems powered by solar cells located on the roof. On one side of the pavilion, water ran continuously down a large glass wall, like a waterfall, evaporating with the heat of the sun and causing a cooling effect. On the other side of the pavilion, large tanks filled with water absorbed heat during the day and cooled down at night, moderating the extreme daily temperatures. The entire building was prefabricated in England and then recycled after the Expo, in keeping with the notion of sustainability.

BUILDING TYPE
● long-span

ENERGY GENERATION
● renewable energy use
● energy conservation systems

LIGHT & AIR
● daylight illumination
● natural ventilation systems
● operable windows

GREENERY, WATER & WASTE
● water conservation and reuse

CONSTRUCTION
● use of renewable materials
● modular construction
techniques
● building reuse

URBANISM
● environmental planning
● public transportation access
● site reuse

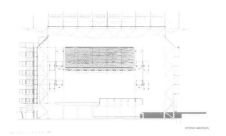

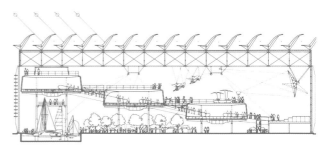

ABOVE **section
showing relationship
between roof canopy and
exhibition areas**

ABOVE **interior showing
water wall beyond and view
of sunscreens and water
containers**

29.

PROJECT
The Eden Project

ARCHITECT
Nicholas Grimshaw
and Partners

LOCATION
St. Austell, England

YEAR
2001

CLIENT
Eden Project Limited

STRUCTURAL ENGINEER
Anthony Hunt Associates

MECHANICAL ENGINEER
ARUP Services Ltd.

CONTRACTOR
McAlpine Joint Venture

The Eden Project rises out of a landscape laid waste by a 37-acre open-pit mine. A botanical garden created to tell the story of how people rely on plants to sustain everyday life, it includes a visitor center and a group of greenhouses called "biomes." Taking advantage of the landscape, the project recycles rain and ground water for irrigation. The walls of the open pit shelter the biomes from the cold. The biomes are made of a material with neither the weight nor the maintenance requirements of glass, which traps heat and enhances plants' exposure to the sun. In the future, the owners of the Eden Project hope to use plant material grown in the biomes to power the building's heating and mechanical systems.

BUILDING TYPE
- long-span

ENERGY GENERATION
- renewable energy use
- energy conservation systems

LIGHT & AIR
- daylight illumination
- natural ventilation systems
- operable windows

GREENERY, WATER & WASTE
- interior and exterior gardens
- water conservation and reuse
- building recycling program

CONSTRUCTION
- use of renewable materials
- use of local or regional materials
- use of low-VOC materials
- modular construction techniques

URBANISM
- environmental planning
- public transportation access
- site reuse

BELOW **site plan showing distribution of biomes and elevation showing relationship of biomes to existing landscape**

OPPOSITE **exterior and interior views of biomes**

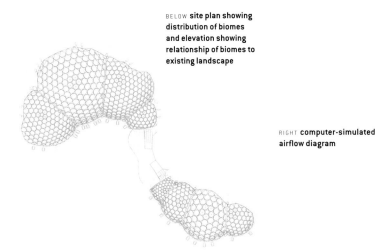

RIGHT **computer-simulated airflow diagram**

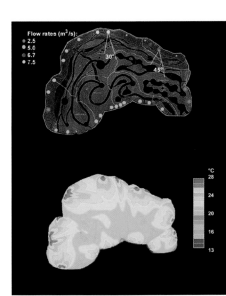

LEFT **detail of glass-pillow connector**

RIGHT **diagram of ventilation and heating strategy**

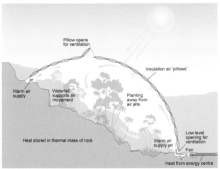

Forest Building – Richmond, Va.
General configuration of landscape and exterior planting.

SITE SSSW-W.
1981

ABOVE **sketch of building concept, James Wines**

OPPOSITE **model showing relationship of trees to building and view of building with tree forecourt**

30. PROJECT
Best Products Company Forest Building

One of a number of big-box retail stores designed by SITE in the late 1970s and early 1980s, the Best Products Company Forest Building outside Richmond, Virginia, remains an example of how anonymous commercial structures can be enlivened by local ecosystems. The architects' design preserved most of the site's existing vegetation, allowing the surrounding forest to envelop and penetrate the structure. A 35-foot space behind the street facade accommodates giant oak trees that shade the central area, reduce water run-off, and promote soil retention.

ARCHITECT
SITE Projects, Inc.

LOCATION
Henrico County, Virginia

YEAR
1980

CLIENT
Best Products

STRUCTURAL ENGINEER
Weidlinger Associates

MECHANICAL &
ELECTRICAL ENGINEER
La Prade Brothers

LANDSCAPE
Watkins Nurseries

CONTRACTOR
Whiting Turner, Inc.

BUILDING TYPE
• long-span

GREENERY, WATER & WASTE
• interior and exterior gardens
• water conservation and reuse

URBANISM
• environmental planning

LEFT **water wall, view of vegetated columns from interior, and vegetated roof**

RIGHT **axonometric sketch, James Wines**

OPPOSITE **daytime and nighttime views of project**

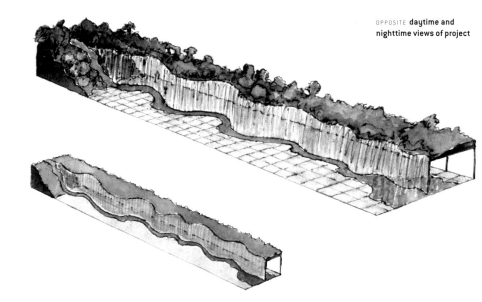

31.

PROJECT
Avenue V, Expo '92

Conceived as a resting place and a link to the Expo '92 pavilions, this project includes a central station for a monorail train and three restaurants. A massive, undulating, glass water wall supports large canopies of vegetation and elevated gardens. The exhibition areas and the monorail station are sheltered by the water wall and shaded by lifted vegetation, tall trees, and a vine-covered trellis. The shape of Avenue V mimics the topography of the Guadalquivir River of Seville, celebrating its history as the route to the sea for fifteenth-century explorers and serving as an example of architecture as a system of climate control.

ARCHITECT
SITE Projects, Inc.

LOCATION
Seville, Spain

YEAR
1992

CLIENT
EXPO '92, 1992 Universal Exposition

ASSOCIATE ARCHITECT
CYGSA Control Y Geologia, S.A.

LANDSCAPE ARCHITECT
Signe Nielsen, P.C.

CONSULTING ENGINEER
Saincosa, S.A.

CONTRACTOR
Ferrovial

BUILDING TYPE
● long-span

ENERGY GENERATION
● energy conservation systems

LIGHT & AIR
● daylight illumination
● natural ventilation systems

GREENERY, WATER & WASTE
● water conservation and reuse
● interior and exterior gardens

CONSTRUCTION
● use of local or regional materials

URBANISM
● environmental planning
● mixed-use building
● public transportation access
● site reuse

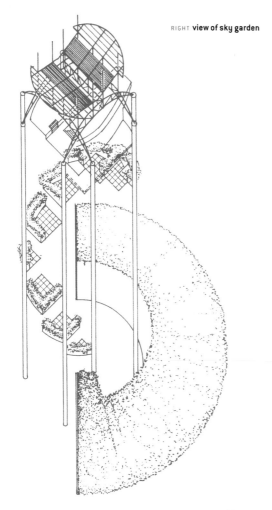

RIGHT **view of sky garden**

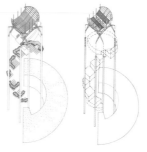
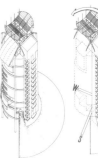
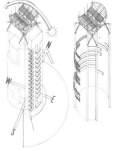

ABOVE **axonometric diagrams of environmental strategies**

OPPOSITE **view of building showing sky gardens and sunscreens**

32. PROJECT
Menara Mesiniaga

Menara Mesiniaga represents a culmination of T.R. Hamzah and Yeang's early research on bioclimatic design in tall buildings. All of the windows facing east and west (the hot sides of the building) have external louvers to reduce solar heat gain. The north and south sides have unshielded windows, improving natural light. The elevator lobbies are naturally ventilated and illuminated, and a roof structure was designed to accommodate photovoltaic panels in the future. But of all the bioclimatic features, the vertical land-scaping is the most representative of T.R. Hamzah and Yeang's approach. Employed in many of the firm's buildings, it is used here on different floors in a staggered or spiral pattern, allowing the plants to receive maximum sunlight and rainwater. The vegetation cools the building and provides workers with a sense of connection to the outdoors and nature.

ARCHITECT
T.R. Hamzah and Yeang, Sdn. Bhd.

LOCATION
Selangor, Malaysia

YEAR
1992

CLIENT
Mesiniaga, Sdn. Bhd.

STRUCTURAL ENGINEER
Reka Perunding

MECHANICAL ENGINEER
Norman Disney and Young

CONTRACTOR
Siah Bros.

BUILDING TYPE
● high-rise

ENERGY GENERATION
● energy conservation systems

LIGHT & AIR
● daylight illumination
● natural ventilation systems

GREENERY, WATER & WASTE
● interior and exterior gardens
● water conservation and reuse

URBANISM
● environmental planning
● site reuse

106

For a building of its size and height, the EDITT Tower has an unprecedented ratio of outdoor planted areas to indoor office spaces. The green spaces ascend from the ground to the top floors, and incorporate vegetation from surrounding landscapes to create ecological continuity. In addition to the greenery, which aids in cooling, air quality, and water maintenance (by filtering rainwater and serving as a site for sewage composting), the building contains a water-recycling, water-purification, and sewage-recycling system. As a result, it uses half as much water as most buildings its size.

ARCHITECT
T.R. Hamzah and Yeang, Sdn. Bhd.

LOCATION
Singapore

YEAR
1998–

CLIENT
Urban Redevelopment Authority, Singapore

STRUCTURAL & MECHANICAL ENGINEER
Battle McCarthy Consulting Engineers & Landscape Architects

BUILDING TYPE
- high-rise

ENERGY GENERATION
- renewable energy use
- energy conservation systems

LIGHT & AIR
- daylight illumination
- natural ventilation systems
- operable windows

GREENERY, WATER & WASTE
- interior and exterior gardens

CONSTRUCTION
- use of local or regional materials
- modular construction techniques

URBANISM
- environmental planning
- public transportation access
- site reuse

RIGHT **photographs of model showing greenery and rainwater catchments**

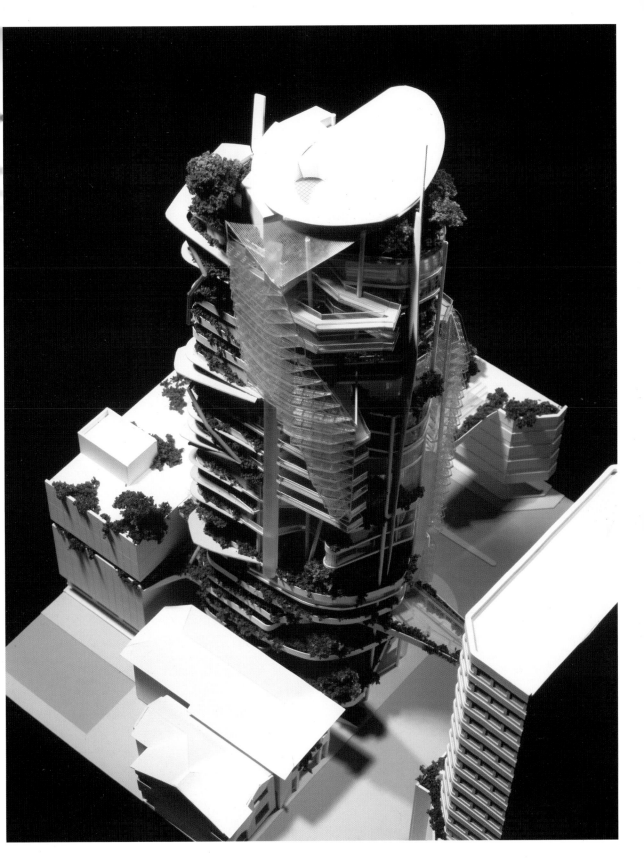

34.

PROJECT
901 Cherry Offices, Corporate Campus

Among its many environmentally sensitive features—roof ventilators, under-floor air, operable windows—the Gap headquarters in San Bruno boasts the largest habitat roof in the United States. Typical large, low-rise office buildings have metal or synthetic rubber roofs, often covered with gravel. The water that runs off them absorbs the toxic chemicals in the roof structure, releasing them into the local water system or soil. Habitat roofs contain soil, grasses, and other vegetation that retain and filter water. They also create a place for birds and native plants, allowing office buildings and local wildlife to coexist.

BUILDING DESIGNER
William McDonough + Partners

EXECUTIVE & INTERIOR ARCHITECT
Gensler

LOCATION
San Bruno, California

YEAR
1996

CLIENT
Gap, Inc.

STRUCTURAL & MECHANICAL ENGINEER
ARUP Services Ltd.

LANDSCAPE ARCHITECT
Hargreaves Associates

CONTRACTOR
Swinerton & Walberg with Fisher Developments, Inc.

BUILDING TYPE
● low-rise

ENERGY GENERATION
● renewable energy use
● energy conservation systems

LIGHT & AIR
● daylight illumination
● natural ventilation systems
● monitored air quality
● operable windows

GREENERY, WATER & WASTE
● interior or exterior gardens
● water conservation systems
● water-reclamation systems
● building recycling program

CONSTRUCTION
● use of renewable materials
● use of local or regional materials
● use of low-VOC materials

URBANISM
● environmental planning

ABOVE **view of project showing habitat roof and ventilators**

LEFT **section**

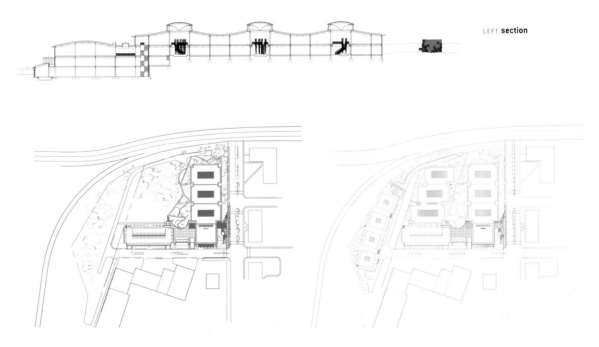

ABOVE **site plans showing current project and future construction**

ARCHITECT
William McDonough +
Partners with
McDonough Braungart
Design Chemistry

LOCATION
Dearborn, Michigan

YEAR
2001–

CLIENT
Ford Motor Company,
Vehicle Operations, Ford
Motor Land Development
Corporation

ARCHITECT & ENGINEER
OF RECORD
Arcadis Giffels

LANDSCAPE ARCHITECT
Susan Nelson-Warren
Byrd Landscape
Architects with D.I.R.T.
Studio

MECHANICAL ENGINEER
Professional Supply, Inc.

Originally designed by Albert Kahn in 1929 and immortalized as a symbol of industrialization, the Ford Factory now stands to become a symbol of environmentalism. In a renovation and addition to the factory, William McDonough + Partners has designed what will be the largest habitat roof and greenery-infused walls in the world. The factory buildings' green roof, combined with other landscaping strategies, will provide natural storm water management, potentially saving Ford millions of dollars.

BUILDING TYPE
● long-span

ENERGY GENERATION
● renewable energy use
● energy conservation systems

LIGHT & AIR
● daylight illumination
● natural ventilation systems
● monitored air quality

GREENERY, WATER & WASTE
● exterior gardens
● water conservation and reuse
● building recycling program

CONSTRUCTION
● use of local or regional materials
● use of low-VOC materials
● building reuse

URBANISM
● environmental planning
● site reuse

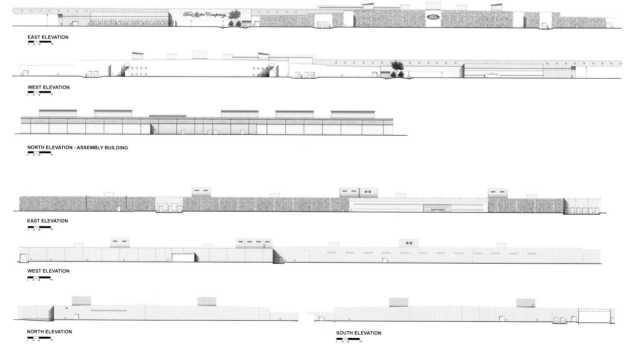

EAST ELEVATION

WEST ELEVATION

NORTH ELEVATION - ASSEMBLY BUILDING

EAST ELEVATION

WEST ELEVATION

NORTH ELEVATION

SOUTH ELEVATION

OPPOSITE site section and elevations showing landscaping and green walls and roofs

ABOVE rendering of factory with plantings

BELOW computer rendering of factory interior showing daylight illumination

Beyond the Limits of Sustainable Architecture:
A New Material Sensibility for the Twenty- first Century

by Michael Braungart

During the last decade of the twentieth century the high-rise building trades were booming. The traditional leaders in skyscraper construction, the urban centers of Europe and North America, were erecting tall building after tall building, reshaping the cityscape in typically energetic fashion. But the real boom was happening elsewhere. In Asia, nearly 1,800 skyscrapers were constructed during the 1990s, making the region the busiest builder of large-scale structures in the world. In Shanghai alone, where in 1969 there were only a dozen high-rises, 138 steel-and-concrete towers transformed the skyline in a single decade.

One might applaud these stunning feats of engineering. The recent building boom in East Asia transformed hundreds of thousands of tons of raw steel into dozens of potent symbols of technology, prosperity, and progress, celebrating the dynamism — short-lived, it turned out — of a late-twentieth-century economic force, the so-called Asian tigers. Yet these new skyscrapers also symbolized many of the environmental problems that have come to define contemporary building design. And they are only a fraction of massive stock of large-scale buildings that grows daily in industrialized nations and at an ever-quickening pace in the developing world.

So what's the problem with large-scale architecture? It's not just

Shanghai, China, 2002

that buildings have gotten so big—it's more complex than that. We are quite capable of designing big, majestic, and inspiring buildings that celebrate human creativity and pleasure with enthusiasm *and* environmental sensitivity. Nevertheless, on a global scale, the physical impact of increasing building mass is undeniable. As we move into the second century of the skyscraper, the construction of buildings is consuming some *three billion tons* of raw materials each year. By most estimates, new construction accounts for 40 percent of the raw stone, gravel, and sand used each year; 40 percent of the processed materials, such as steel; and one-quarter of the world's wood harvest. Together, new and existing buildings account for two-fifths of the world's annual energy use, one-sixth of its water consumption, and one-half of its waste stream. In fact, the construction and maintenance of modern buildings rivals the material and energy use of the entire manufacturing sector of the global economy.[1]

This gargantuan appetite for raw materials results in some of the same problems associated with the production and consumption of consumer goods. Office towers, like industrial processes, are powered by fossil fuels and nuclear reactors. Their wastes pile up in landfills and pollute the air, water, and soil. Through material supply chains that span the world, the impact of buildings extends well beyond their local footprint. An architect's choice of materials in Manhattan, for example, triggers a series of events halfway around the globe in Madagascar or Brazil. Depending on the material—it might be raw gravel for cheap concrete, a rare, precious cabinet wood, or iron ore for steel beams—an architect's *uninformed* choices might contribute in some small way to deforestation, an increase in toxic mine tailings, or the loss of biological and cultural diversity. A preponderance of uninformed choices has led to the slow unraveling of the web of life.

An architect's material choices also influence human health. Beyond the widespread environmental problems that undermine social well-being, the various ingredients that go into a building also have invisible, long-term effects on both building occupants and those who manufacture and dispose of architectural materials. Indeed, *none* of the materials used to make large-scale buildings is specifically designed to be healthful for people. Even a cursory inventory begins to suggest some of the challenges architects are now facing.

Consider, for example, the ubiquitous use of polyvinyl chloride. Polyvinyl chloride, better known as PVC or vinyl, is a common ingredient in windows, doors, flooring, wall-coverings, interior surfaces, and insulating materials. Many formulations of PVC have

view of logging operation

view of mining operation

1. David Malin Roodman and Nicholas Lenssen, *A Building Revolution: How Ecology and Health Concerns Are Transforming Construction* (Washington, DC: Worldwatch Institute, 1995), 23.

been known to contain toxic heavy metals that are carcinogenic and endocrine disrupting. Equally common are formaldehyde (a reproductive toxin found in particleboard, paints, and textiles) and other volatile organic compounds (VOCs), some of which are suspected carcinogens and immune-system disrupters that are used in adhesives and carpets. Formaldehyde and VOCs seep, or off-gas, from architectural materials, accumulating in tightly sealed buildings in concentrations that make indoor air quality on average three times worse than the most noxious urban air. Design flaws that trap moisture in buildings add mold to the list of substances fouling indoor air. This forced flow of chemicals and molds through inadequate ventilation systems adds up to the costly health problems associated with Sick Building syndrome, which affects more than 30 percent of new and renovated buildings worldwide. Some energy-efficient buildings, which are designed to require less heating and cooling, and thus less air circulation, only make things worse. Fortunately, an expanding palette of materials is allowing designers to phase out the use of PVC and other toxic substances, a promising step for twenty-first century architecture.

The Building as Machine

Many of these problems with building mass and materials can be traced to aesthetics. "The house is a machine for living in," Le Corbusier famously said.[2] Writing and working in the early and mid-twentieth century, Le Corbusier and the other modernists such as Walter Gropius and Mies van der Rohe pursued a rational, minimalist approach to architecture to free it from class distinctions and the nationalist ideologies of the day. They employed modern materials, new technology, and industrial forms (the building as a sleek, mass-produced machine) in the interest of replacing unsanitary, inequitable housing with clean, austere buildings for the masses. Their theories and their glass-walled high-rises helped articulate a modernist sensibility that came to be known as the International Style. These architects, and those who followed them, designed monuments to rational form and pure function, which to a great degree achieved their end: an international aesthetic largely freed from the constraints and ideologies of particular places.

Out of the aesthetic drive of modernism emerged a new material sensibility and a novel concept of building mass. Modernist architects conceived of buildings as light, rectilinear enclosures of dynamic volumes of space. The robust mass of traditional stone and brick provided a poor representation of this modern idea of form. Instead, the modern architect turned to concrete, steel, and glass, far better materials for suggesting lightness, space,

LEFT **workshops, Bauhaus, Dessau, Germany, Walter Gropius, 1926**
BELOW **Seagram Building, New York City, Ludwig Mies van der Rohe, 1958**

2. Le Corbusier, *Towards a New Architecture* (New York: Dover, 1986), 4.

transparency, and sleek, industrial modernity.

In his early career, Le Corbusier was especially drawn to glass. As Reyner Banham writes, "all other materials seem to have been in his eyes poor substitutes for glass, his ideal of the de-materialised building skin. . . ."[3] Yet Le Corbusier and others after him were to find glass walls a mixed blessing. Consider his Cité de Refuge: When the Salvation Army hostel opened in December of 1933, the building's south-facing, multistory, sealed glass wall offered, as Le Corbusier wrote, "the ineffable joys" of sunlight and warmth on a cold winter day.[4] When summer rolled around, however, the ineffable sunlight made the tightly sealed Cité de Refuge an unbearable hothouse, a problem that could only be addressed with another emerging technology of the day, air-conditioning.

Called "man-made weather" by its inventor, Willis Carrier, air-conditioning liberated modern architecture from nature.[5] It allowed Le Corbusier to dream of "one single building for all nations and climates," the machinelike structure independent of place.[6] With a few notable exceptions, his dream has come true. If we scan the skyline of Shanghai we see little that is much different from the skylines of Los Angeles, Manhattan, or Frankfurt. The buildings are steel-and-glass boxes, tightly sealed, short on fresh air and natural light, their internal ecosystems divorced from their surroundings.

If buildings such as these were to be a strike against nationalism, they have become as well a leveler of cultural diversity, overshadowing the very rich differences between Eastern and Western approaches to shelter and landscape. Tracing the influences of modernism, we can begin to see how architectural form influences culture, and how material sensibilities and design issues raise serious cultural questions. And this is where today's architects might want to be careful and humble. Developing new designs in response to cultural issues is not always a very clear process. The mid-twentieth-century modernists were very aware that they were involved in a cultural struggle, yet this did not necessarily help them achieve positive cultural ends. In 1950s Berlin, for example, architecture was a key signifier of political identity. East German communists thought modernism was decadent and useless—the skyscraper was seen as a cathedral of capitalism—while the modernists believed their work symbolized an enlightened, egalitarian alternative to Stalinism. Ironically, no skyscrapers were built in West Berlin during the Cold War, while in East Berlin mammoth TV towers became the tallest structures in Europe. Nonetheless, as James Howard Kunstler writes, Stalin's hatred of modernist buildings actually empowered modernism in the West, where it became "the architecture disliked by fascists and

RIGHT **New National Gallery, Berlin, Germany, Ludwig Mies van der Rohe, 1965**
BELOW **New York City skyline**

3. Reyner Banham, *The Architecture of the Well-Tempered Environment* (London: Architectural P., 1969), 154–55.

4. Le Corbusier in Banham, 157.

5. Banham, 172.

6. Le Corbusier in Banham, 169.

communists, and therefore the official architecture of democracy and human decency."[7]

But human dignity was not aided by modernism in either East or West Berlin. "Perversely," Kunstler continues, "postwar West Berlin, the island of liberty in a sea of socialist oppression, became a showcase of monumental Bauhaus-inspired modernism composed of intrinsically despotic buildings that made people feel placeless, powerless, insignificant, and less than human."[8]

Not what one would hope for from the architecture of human decency. Unfortunately, the landscape of West Berlin—a landscape of machines for living designed for all nations and climates, but not specifically for West Berlin—is being repeated with great regularity around the world, undermining not only the health of the land, soil, air, and water, but the very real human need to take pleasure in the designs and materials of the built environment and the natural world. We can do far better.

Dematerialization: A New Take on an Old Perspective
A new generation of architects has set its mind on just that. After years of brutish resource extraction and energy use, designers of large-scale buildings are becoming aware of a new sensibility that links architecture to environmental concerns. Many are trying

to address the negative effects of buildings with designs and practices that use energy and materials more efficiently.

This shift among architects has emerged in the context of a wider movement toward resource efficiency associated with a desire for sustainable development. Sustainability is a slippery and not very descriptive term, but it is often used to describe efforts to integrate social and environmental concerns with the more carnivorous aspects of the global economy, making commerce more viable over the long term. One of its goals is the decoupling of material use from economic growth, which is essentially a strategy of doing more with less in an increasingly crowded world. A report by the World Resources Institute, for example, projects a 300 percent rise in energy and material use as world population and economic activity increase over the next 50 years. As long as economic growth implies an increase in material use, the study warns, "there is little hope of limiting the impacts of human activity on the natural environment." But, the report continues, if industry can become more efficient, using less material to provide the goods and services people want, economic growth can be sustained, thus decoupled from resource extraction and environmental harm.[9]

Translated into practice, this idea is often called eco-efficiency—a leading business strategy in the 1990s that influenced

FAR LEFT **Potsdamer Platz, Berlin, Germany, 1999**
LEFT **CBS Building, New York City, Eero Saarinen, 1965**

7. James Howard Kunstler, *The City in Mind: Meditations on the Urban Condition* (New York: Free Press, 2001), 128.

8. Kunstler, 129.

9. Jonathan Lash et al. in Emily Matthews, *The Weight of Nations: Material Outflows from Industrial Economies* (Washington, DC: World Resources Institute, 2000).

architecture as well. Eco-efficient businesses try to release less waste into the air, send less material to the landfill, and make fewer dangerous chemicals. "Reduce, reuse, recycle" is eco-efficiency's popular mantra. Architects influenced by eco-efficiency follow a similar path. Many try to do more with less by reducing the energy consumption of buildings.

Designers of eco-efficient buildings employ a variety of tools to minimize energy use. Typically, big energy-savers are heavily insulated and tightly sealed to minimize heat and cooling loss and to reduce the need for air filtration. Dark tinted glass or coated "superwindows" that emit light but reflect heat can lower solar income, diminish the building's demand on its air-conditioning system, and thereby cut fossil-fuel consumption. The local power plant, in turn, releases a smaller amount of pollutants into the environment, cutting emissions of particulate matter and greenhouse gasses.

Formal innovations are sometimes combined with new materials to make big buildings more resource efficient. Edificio Malecon, a 125,000-square-foot office building in Buenos Aires, for example, was designed to minimize the heat of the sun by pinching its long, narrow mass on the east and west ends and using sunshades to screen its broad northern and southern exposures. Together, these

innovations are said to "virtually eliminate direct solar radiation during peak cooling months."[10]

Recycling building materials and retrofitting building mass are techniques also being employed to reduce the environmental impact of large-scale structures. The renovation of the Audubon Society's offices in a 100-year-old building in Manhattan preserved 300 tons of steel, 9,000 tons of masonry, and 560 tons of concrete while making the building a model of high-tech energy efficiency.[11] Projects such as this suggest both the typically unseen potential of the current building stock and the need to construct new buildings for multiple uses in the future. As an emerging market for recycled glass, sheetrock, carpeting, and reusable high-quality construction materials grows more stable, buildings and materials with many lives may become more the rule than the exception.

Other approaches take direct aim at reducing resource consumption by simply using less material to make things. Dematerialization, as this strategy is often called, is the materialist's way to efficiency. One of its leading proponents is Adriaan Beukers, professor of composite materials and structures at Delft University of Technology. Beukers, a former rocket-materials scientist, is intrigued by lightweight structures and the possibilities of getting maximum performance from minimum materials. His premise is

RIGHT **Edificio Malecon, Buenos Aires, Argentina, Hellmuth, Obata + Kassabaum, 1999**
FAR RIGHT **National Audubon Society, New York City, Croxton Collaborative, Architects, 1992**

10. Kira Gould, "COTE Top 10 Green Projects for 2002," *AIArchitect*, May 2002, 4.

11. National Audubon Society, *Audubon Headquarters: Building for an Environmental Future* (New York: National Audubon Society, 1991), 6.

simple: Lightweight, fiber-reinforced composite materials, intelligently composed, can yield structural strength while dramatically cutting resource consumption.

Beuker's "minimum energy structures" are inspired by the tools and shelters carried by ancient nomadic people, which had to be light for easy transport. They were made of natural polymers, such as bone or skin, or composites such as straw and mud. Fast forward to the twenty-first century: With energy resources in decline, Beukers says, we have to remember how to travel and build light. Today's synthetic composites (layered textiles woven with carbon fibers and resin, for example) give us the technology to do so. Composite materials are already being applied to new products, such as windmill rotor blades and lightweight beer kegs that deflate after use, saving transportation costs and valuable steel.[12]

Beukers thinks this is the future of architectural materials, too. He sees inflatable buildings made of strong, flexible composites; textiles molded into prefab materials; Bucky Fuller–style structures relying on the relationship between tension and compression; and, harking back to ancient design, structures inspired by the tensile strength of tents. We already see "tensegrity" applied to our domed stadiums, and architects such as Renzo Piano often use tentlike roofing. Some believe "a culture of 'lightness' is beginning to take root," seeing in its emerging influence a "key to apprehending the relationship between design and sustainability."[13]

Do these approaches to sustainability—efficiency, recycling, dematerialization, lightness—signal the decoupling of materials from economic growth that the World Resources Institute is hoping for? Perhaps. Does that mean we can now begin to feel more sanguine about architecture's effect on nature and human culture? Well, maybe not.

Each of these strategies has something to offer. Certainly, retrofitting an old building and reusing materials is a positive way to create new, pleasant spaces for office workers. And it's true that efficiently constructed buildings cut waste, and that light materials minimize resource consumption. But the overall design and material makeup of efficient buildings is very much like that of the skyscrapers of Shanghai and Berlin. While their designers may make material substitutions—superglass, triple glazing, recycled plastic surfaces—the chemistry of materials in efficient buildings tends to be largely the same as that in both their predecessors and their more gluttonous contemporaries. The same carcinogens, the same toxic heavy metals, the same endocrine disrupters—only now more tightly enclosed. Are these the kind of buildings we want all over the world?

Carlos Mosley Music Pavilion during assembly, Central Park, New York City, FTL Design Engineering Studio, 1992

12. Adriaan Beukers and Ed van Hinte, *Lightness: The Inevitable Renaissance of Minimum Energy Structures* (Rotterdam: 010 Publishers, 1998).

13. Oliver Lowenstein, "Lightness and Industry," *Unstructured* (www.fourthdoor.co.uk/unstructured/lightness2.html), April 9, 2002.

Recycling, too, can be problematic. Most recycling is actually downcycling, with materials losing value as they circulate through industrial systems. When plastics are recycled into countertops, for example, valuable materials are mixed and can't be recycled again; their trip to the landfill has only been slowed down. The same is true of Beukers's ultralight composite materials; they are hybrids right from the start and can't be recycled effectively even once.

That may not sound terribly troubling in these times, but mixing construction materials not designed to be recycled can be quite destructive. The strength of steel, for instance, is compromised when it is mixed with other metals in the recycling process. Nevertheless, low-grade steel made from recycled American automobiles is often used for construction overseas. Recycled steel from the U.S. and Europe is used for building construction in Asia, and its wide use in Turkey may have been responsible for the collapse of so many buildings during the earthquake that rocked the country in 1999.

Mixing metals dilutes their value and increases the impact of materials. When rare and valuable metals such as copper, nickel, and manganese are blended in the recycling process, their discrete value is lost forever. Creating new stockpiles is extraordinarily costly. Mining and processing one ton of copper, for example,

creates 600 tons of industrial waste.

A materials passport, much like the bar code on consumer goods, could change that. The passport would essentially guide materials through industrial cycles, routing them from production through reuse, defining optimum uses and intelligent practices. Valuable copper would remain available for use as valuable copper, not just one of many ingredients in hybrid products of lesser value. New recycling processes can even add value to materials as they flow through the cycles of industry.

At issue in today's practice of sustainable architecture are not the good intentions of all those trying to make a difference by doing things efficiently. It is simply that efficiency as a goal, as an end in itself, does not address the fundamental flaws in building design. Sometimes it makes things worse. Efficiency falls short, not because it does not cut or limit or minimize enough, but because it is utterly defined by limitations: Seeking to be merely sustainable, one arrives at a minimum condition for survival—not a very inspiring prospect.

A New Relation to Materials

Imagine a factory or office building that celebrates the abundance of nature's material wealth rather than bemoaning its shortage. By

clearly understanding the chemistry of natural processes and their interactions with human purpose, not only can we imagine such places, we can build them. This suggests a radical shift from designing large-scale buildings as inanimate, one-size-fits-all objects into which we plug power and largely toxic materials, to designing buildings as life-support systems embedded in the material and energy flows of particular places. It's a design strategy animated by ecological intelligence.

Ecologically intelligent design seeks not efficiency but rematerialization. Rematerialization can be understood as both a metaphor and a process. In the industrial world, it refers to chemical recycling that adds value to materials, allowing them to be used again and again in high-quality products. The process is modeled on nature's nutrient and energy systems, which perpetually recycle materials in closed-loop cycles. Industrial ecology applies the structure of these natural systems to the management of industry's material flows, so that all products and materials, after their useful commercial lives, can be returned to the soil or circulated in industry forever.

Applied to architecture, rematerialization describes both a relationship to materials informed by natural systems and a layered strategy for redesigning the chemistry of large-scale buildings. The key to effective rematerialization—and to ecologically intelligent architecture—is not limiting mass or reducing energy consumption, but designing healthful materials that can safely circulate in closed-loop cycles and integrating nature's own nutrient and energy systems into building design. The goal is not less impact, but more—life-supporting structures that leave a big, positive ecological footprint: more habitat, more clean water, more fresh air, more pleasure, more beauty, more biological and cultural diversity, more fun.

Ecological intelligence begins with material chemistry. We are only beginning to understand the effects of the chemicals we live with every day in our homes and workplaces, and each year, approximately 2,000 new chemicals are introduced worldwide without any need for approval. The toxicological data simply can't keep up. Through existing chemical assessments, however, we do know enough to begin to select materials that are safe, and even beneficial, for human and environmental health.

Consider insulation. It's not the most visible or exciting material on the block but it's crucial to both health and performance in large- and small-scale buildings. The typical palette includes insulation made from fiberglass, rigid foam, cellulose, or polyurethane—all of which contain problematic substances. The resins in batt insulation

OPPOSITE **rice-husk harvesting and BASF nylon carpet, McDonough Braungart Design Chemistry, 2001**

contain formaldehyde; rigid foam contains organohalogens, which are toxic, or styrene, a carcinogen; and cellulose contains reproductive toxins. But there are alternatives. Rice-husk insulation and rice straw, for example, are achieving market viability: They are safe, effective, inexpensive, totally biodegradable, and produced with a renewable resource that does not displace a food crop.

As harvesting rice husks suggests, the various effects of materials extend from the molecule to the region, from a particular building and its inhabitants to the human settlements and natural systems in which they are embedded. Materials harvested intelligently tend to preserve rather than damage the economic, environmental, and social assets of communities near and far. Wood products certified by the Forest Stewardship Council, for example, must be harvested following well-defined principles that protect biological diversity, honor the rights and knowledge of indigenous people, and respect the need to carefully manage working forests. The principles, in essence, aim to enhance a wide spectrum of community wealth, and they begin to suggest the ecosystem perspective that underlies ecologically intelligent design.

With an ecological perspective, a material life cycle begins to emerge. Typically, the life cycle of a product consists of a one-way trip to the landfill or incinerator. But when a product has a safe,

positively defined material chemistry, it can flow in a closed-loop, cradle-to-cradle life cycle, providing nourishment for nature or infinitely recyclable materials for industry. Just as in nature, when the byproducts of one organism become food for another, the flow of these biological nutrients and technical nutrients in their respective cycles eliminates the concept of waste.

We don't have to settle for imagining cradle-to-cradle architectural materials; they already exist. An upholstery fabric I designed with William McDonough as a biological nutrient abrades safe fibers rather than off-gassing toxicity, and will decompose after its useful life. BASF, the commercial carpet company, has developed a system to transform old nylon carpet fiber into the highest quality yarn without any significant loss of material. The process adds value to the old nylon rather than downcycling it into a product of lower quality. That's rematerialization, not dematerialization. Or reincarnation—a material coming back into existence at a higher level of evolution.

Life-cycle thinking becomes truly effective within the conceptual framework of intelligent building systems, such as those being developed by the architectural researchers Volker Hartkopf and Vivian Loftness of Carnegie Mellon University in Pittsburgh. Hartkopf founded the Center for Building Performance and Diagnostics,

where he has developed a consortium of 42 building-industry partners conducting research on new construction technologies, from raised-access floor systems to skylights for daylighting, recyclable carpets to sustainable seating. Perhaps as important as the actual technical advances is the emerging framework for cooperation between industry leaders, researchers, and architects. Hartkopf's success at advancing research within partner companies suggests the real possibility of establishing cooperative systems for the industry-wide tracking, retrieval, and reuse of architectural materials.

Together, Hartkopf and Loftness conceived the idea for the Robert L. Preger Intelligent Workplace, a model of smart systems applied to passive strategies of climate control in office buildings. Previous research had led them to conclude, Hartkopf told *Architecture* magazine, that conventional office buildings were inadequate "if they were measured through the eyes, noses, and ears of the occupants."[14] Seeking an alternative, the Intelligent Workplace is designed to use technology to create a high level of personal health and comfort. A system of intelligent indoor-outdoor sensors monitors temperature, air quality, wind speed, and humidity, making the building incredibly responsive to its environment. A central computer system tapped into the sensors

lights the building as needed and optimizes flows of air, daylight, shading, and radiant heat, handling most of the climate-control load. This marriage of high and low tech effectively enmeshes the building in local energy flows, tapping into the surroundings to the advantage of all its inhabitants. Intelligent indeed.

Ultimately, that's what guides ecologically intelligent design— an openness and attention to place that allows one to discover fitting materials, fitting forms, and fitting systems, so that human habitation supports the life of a locale. Combining this local knowledge with an understanding of intelligent materials and energy systems, architects can create buildings that encourage healthy interaction with the natural environment.

The Adam Joseph Lewis Center for Environmental Studies at Oberlin College, designed by William McDonough + Partners, is such a building. In fact, the Lewis Center fits in its surroundings like a tree in the forest: Enmeshed in local energy flows, it accrues solar energy, makes oxygen, filters water, and creates a healthy habitat for living things. Geothermal wells heat and cool the building. A constructed marsh-like ecosystem breaks down and digests organic material and releases clean water. The fabrics used for upholstery are biological nutrients, and the carpeting can be recycled when it wears out. The surrounding landscape provides

Robert L. Preger Intelligent Workplace, Carnegie Mellon University, Pittsburgh, Center for Building Performance and Diagnostics, 1995–1997

14. Ann C. Sullivan, "Academic Initiative," *Architecture*, May 1998.

social gathering spaces, instructional gardens, and a newly planted forest grove, which is reestablishing the habitat of the building's northern Ohio location. Inside and out, the Lewis Center is becoming entwined with its place, teaching day to day how to mindfully engage the world.

There is still a long way to go. Architects have just begun, really, to assess materials, determine their problems, assets, and positive effects, and design new ecologically intelligent materials that flow in cradle-to-cradle cycles. Perhaps there will come a day when all building materials have passports that enable architects and builders to quickly assess their material chemistry and life-cycle potential. That would turn a process that is quite arduous into a pleasurable investigation into the history and future of a material: Where has it come from? How was it harvested? How did it get here? Where is it bound at the end of its life? The answers to those questions would tell a very rich story about the many ways in which we shape our world. I can't imagine not wanting to know, or wanting less material to wonder about.

Why not create buildings and systems that give more people more of what they want, need, and love? Cradle-to-cradle materials allow us to do so. And intelligent buildings allow us to leave an ever-larger ecological footprint, an imprint on the world that we can delight in rather than lament. Ultimately, it will be the delight buildings inspire, the way they enhance our feeling for life, that will move ecologically intelligent design from the agenda of a few to the demand of many. Imagine buildings so delightful, so expressive of the world's diverse interactions between nature and human culture, so comfortably affordable for so many, so able to inspire wonder in the living world, that the demand for them is driven by pleasure from the bottom up. Then perhaps, the newest skyscraper in Shanghai will be powered locally and remotely by the wind and the sun, and on a stroll down a wide, sunlit hallway you will feel a breeze from the East China Sea and know quite certainly just where you are and how it feels to inhabit that unique coastal land.

Michael Braungart is founder of the Environmental Protection Encouragement Agency in Hamburg, Germany, and cofounder of McDonough Braungart Design Chemistry in Charlottesville, Virginia.

Adam Joseph Lewis Center for Environmental Studies, Oberlin College, Oberlin, Ohio, William McDonough + Partners, 2000

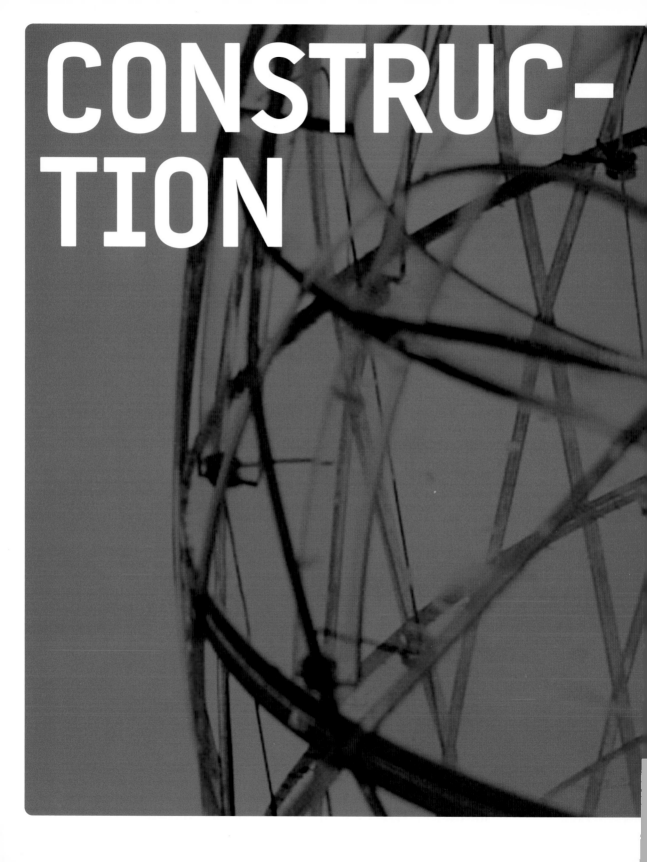

CONSTRUC-
TION

The materials used to construct large-scale buildings—concrete, steel, wood, plastics—all create environmental problems because of the energy used to fabricate them and the toxic chemicals that make them attractive, waterproof, or fireproof. Construction methods—including on-site welding, transportation of materials, and the use of raw and uncut materials—only exacerbate the problem by contaminating the building site with pollution, waste, and noise. Some architects and engineers concerned with environmental sensitivity are now using a variety of strategies to limit the environmental impact of building construction. Of course, one of the most obvious solutions is to reuse buildings that already exist. But if that's not possible, architects can use materials that require little energy to produce and ship, and are renewable, modular (to reduce construction waste), and prefabricated (so construction can be done in factories and not on city streets).

36.

National Audubon Society

A virtual recycling of an 1891 George B. Post–designed building, the new headquarters for the National Audubon Society sets a benchmark for sustainable design. Audubon House is eight stories high with a new rooftop conference center and two below-grade levels. The architects reworked the existing building to improve daylighting and energy efficiency. The building uses 64 percent less energy than required by code, has dramatically better indoor air quality, and exemplifies resource conservation. Annual energy savings is estimated to be as much as $100,000 per year.

ARCHITECT
Croxton Collaborative, Architects

LOCATION
New York City

YEAR
1992

CLIENT
National Audubon Society

BUILDING SERVICES ENGINEER
Flack & Kurtz, Inc.

STRUCTURAL ENGINEER
Robert Silman Associates

GENERAL CONTRACTOR
A.J. Contracting Company, Inc.

BUILDING TYPE
- mid-rise

ENERGY GENERATION
- renewable energy use

LIGHT & AIR
- daylight illumination
- monitored air quality
- operable windows

GREENERY, WATER & WASTE
- water conservation and reuse
- building recycling program

CONSTRUCTION
- use of renewable materials
- use of low-VOC materials
- building reuse

URBANISM
- public transportation access
- mixed-use building
- site reuse

ABOVE **view of natural light in office**

OPPOSITE **view of offices**

ABOVE FROM LEFT **view of renovated building, recycled trash chutes, staircase**

ABOVE **views of restored building and work area**

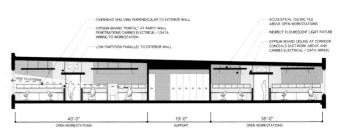

ABOVE **section diagram of environmental strategies**

OPPOSITE **reception area and typical workstation**

37.

Greenpeace U.S.A. Headquarters

The Greenpeace Headquarters sets a high standard for sustainable design in interior office renovations. Issues of natural daylighting, ergonomics, renewable energy generation, and indoor air quality influenced the design process. It was important to Greenpeace that workers' spaces reflect the organization's ideals, so open offices replaced more traditional closed offices, allowing the interiors to receive natural daylight. The architects selected environmentally sensitive building materials and furniture, and incorporated solar cells into the roof to generate energy. The offices are located near a major underground commuter train station and include space for bicycle storage.

ARCHITECT
Envision Design, P.L.L.C.

LOCATION
Washington, DC

YEAR
2000

CLIENT
Greenpeace U.S.A.

BUILDING SERVICES ENGINEER
GHT, Ltd.

STRUCTURAL ENGINEER
Rathgeber/Goss Associates

CONSTRUCTION MANAGER
Mark G. Anderson Consultants

GENERAL CONTRACTOR
Hitt Contracting, Inc.

BUILDING TYPE
• mid-rise

ENERGY GENERATION
• renewable energy use
• energy conservation systems

LIGHT & AIR
• daylight illumination
• natural ventilation systems
• operable windows

GREENERY, WATER & WASTE
• building recycling program

CONSTRUCTION
• use of renewable materials
• use of local or regional materials
• use of low-VOC materials
• building reuse

URBANISM
• public transportation access
• mixed-use building
• site reuse

38

PROJECT
Recyclable, Portable Fabric Skyscraper

ARCHITECT & ENGINEER
FTL Design Engineering
Studio

YEAR
2000 (unbuilt)

When FTL Design Engineering Studio developed the Recyclable, Portable Skyscraper, it wasn't for the typical corporate client who builds to convey an image of permanence. The 12-story office building was conceived with disaster relief agencies, international event managers, and other nomadic office workers in mind. The building, which can be erected in two weeks and requires no foundation, uses a variety of technologies available at most construction sites—portable bathrooms, scaffolding, portable elevators. The trucks at the base can be used to transport the components of the tower and to provide fuel and water for the people who work inside. Unlike other buildings, the Recyclable, Portable Skyscraper can be packed up and reassembled in a different location when it's no longer needed, taking the mantra of "reduce, reuse, recycle" to an entirely new level.

BUILDING TYPE
● high-rise

LIGHT & AIR
● daylight illumination
● natural ventilation systems
● operable windows

GREENERY, WATER & WASTE
● water-reclamation systems

CONSTRUCTION
● use of renewable materials
● modular construction techniques
● building reuse

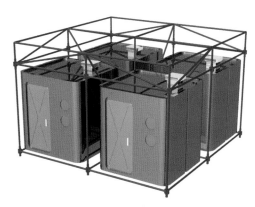

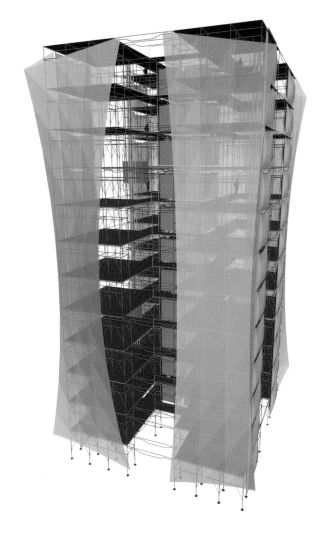

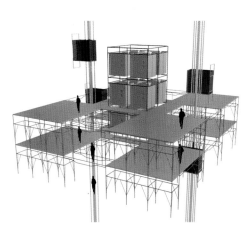

ABOVE **computer renderings of bathroom pods, construction, and facade**

OPPOSITE **project with service trucks**

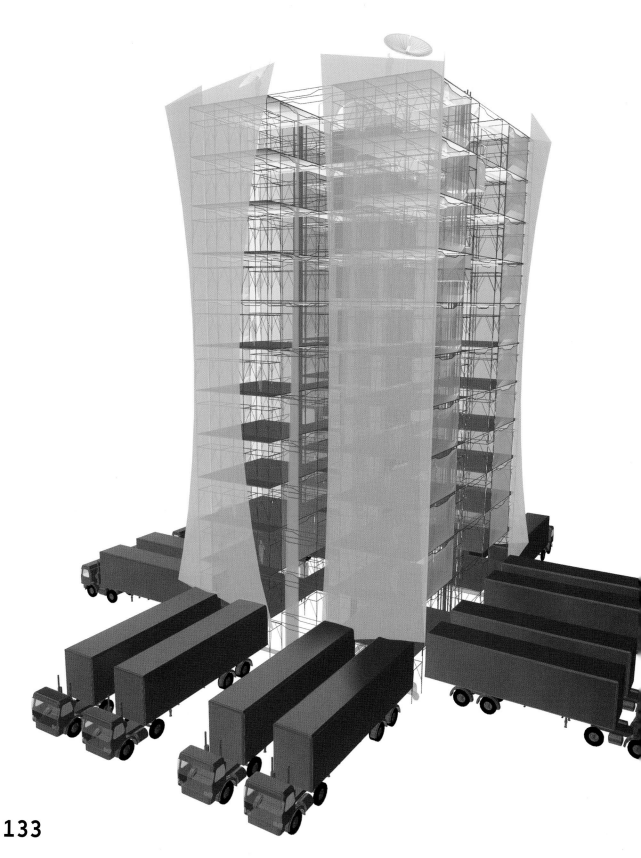

133

39.

Esplanade Condominium Apartments

When Moshe Safdie designed Habitat, he claimed he was not designing a building but creating a housing system based on flexible modules manufactured entirely off site, which could be assembled in different configurations based on local conditions. Habitat remains a visionary system, primarily for its use of prefabricated units and the generous private outdoor space provided for every resident. With the Esplanade Condominium Apartments, Safdie demonstrates how the concepts of Habitat can be realized in a dense setting, using contemporary construction methods. Instead of entirely prefabricated units, the Esplanade uses prefabricated, precast concrete panels and traditional brick veneer in a standard structural concrete frame.

ARCHITECT
Moshe Safdie and Associates, Inc.

LOCATION
Cambridge, Massachusetts

YEAR
1986–1989

CLIENT
Cohen Properties

STRUCTURAL ENGINEER
Robertson, Fowler & Associates

MECHANICAL, ELECTRICAL & PLUMBING ENGINEER
Cosentini Associates

GENERAL CONTRACTOR
Morse Diesel, Inc.

BUILDING TYPE
- high-rise

LIGHT & AIR
- daylight illumination
- natural ventilation systems
- operable windows

GREENERY, WATER & WASTE
- exterior gardens

CONSTRUCTION
- use of renewable materials
- use of local or regional materials
- modular construction techniques

URBANISM
- environmental planning
- public transportation access
- mixed-use building
- site reuse

ABOVE **building section and upper level plan**

BELOW **axonometric of units and terraces and first floor plan**

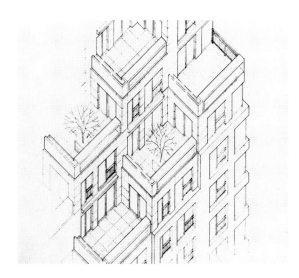

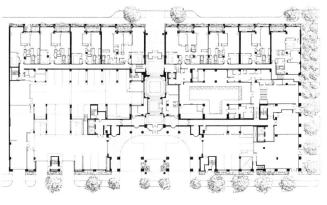

RIGHT **view of building from terraces**
BELOW **view of building from street**

40.

PROJECT
Lloyd's of London

The Lloyd's of London Building—the headquarters for one of the world's oldest insurance companies— has been lauded for its high-tech profile, but it is also an excellent example of environmentally sensitive construction, particularly in its use of modular, prefabricated components that reduced construction waste, on-site construction time, and pollution. The modular concrete frame, glass walls, and service units also resolved tight space restrictions imposed by the medieval streets of the City of London. When services are outdated, they can be easily replaced with new units.

ARCHITECT
Richard Rogers Partnership

LOCATION
London, England

YEAR
1986

CLIENT
Lloyd's of London

STRUCTURAL & MECHANICAL ENGINEER
ARUP Services Ltd.

CONTRACTOR
Bovis Construction Limited

BUILDING TYPE
● high-rise

ENERGY GENERATION
● energy conservation systems

LIGHT & AIR
● daylight illumination
● natural ventilation systems
● operable windows

GREENERY, WATER & WASTE
● water conservation and reuse

CONSTRUCTION
● use of local and regional materials
● modular construction techniques

URBANISM
● public transportation access
● site reuse

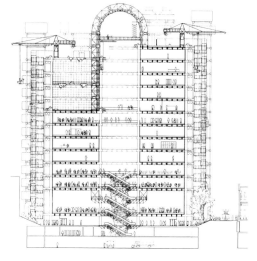

ABOVE **section**

TOP **atrium from above**
CENTER FROM LEFT **curtain wall system, fire stair, and concrete connector**

ABOVE **trading areas**

OPPOSITE **view of building**

136

ARCHITECT
Richard Rogers Partnership

LOCATION
Korea

YEAR
1998 (unbuilt)

CLIENT
Hanseem

STRUCTURAL & MECHANICAL ENGINEER
ARUP Services Ltd.

The Hanseem Corporation commissioned the Richard Rogers Partnership to research the design and manufacture of a high-quality, low-cost housing system for Korea. The goal was to use advanced manufacturing and construction techniques to produce 100,000 fully furnished units at 20 percent of the cost of conventional construction. Standard housing units will be prefabricated and shipped to the site, where they will be erected in various configurations to create a high degree of formal complexity on the steep, densely forested hillsides of the Korean countryside. The system will have little effect on the local environment, as most construction occurs off site; on-site construction involves only minor preparatory work and assembly of the constituent parts.

BUILDING TYPE
- high-rise

ENERGY GENERATION
- energy conservation systems

LIGHT & AIR
- daylight illumination
- natural ventilation systems
- operable windows

CONSTRUCTION
- use of renewable materials
- use of local or regional materials
- modular construction techniques

URBANISM
- environmental planning

BELOW **computer renderings of apartment interior and transformable kitchen area**

BELOW **unit and building fabrication diagrams**

OPPOSITE **photograph of building model**

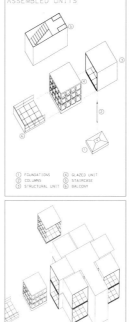

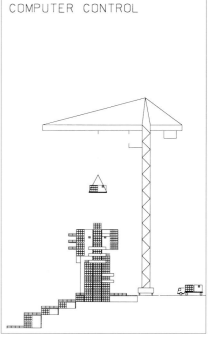

ABOVE **view of exterior**

42. PROJECT
Japan Pavilion

Well known for his houses made of recycled paper tubes, Shigeru Ban took his exploration of paper-tube construction systems to an entirely new level with his Japanese pavilion for Expo 2000. This long-span space was constructed with an undulating mesh of tubes, treated with waterproofing material, and covered with a thin translucent material. The sand-and-stone foundations were recycled for use in other buildings when the pavilion was dismantled.

ARCHITECT
Shigeru Ban

LOCATION
Hannover, Germany

YEAR
2000

CONSULTING ARCHITECT
Frei Otto

STRUCTURAL ENGINEER
Buro Happold Consulting Engineers

BUILDING TYPE
● long-span

LIGHT & AIR
● daylight illumination
● natural ventilation systems

CONSTRUCTION
● use of renewable materials
● use of local or regional materials
● use of low-VOC materials
● modular construction techniques

URBANISM
● environmental planning
● public transportation access

ABOVE **view of interior**

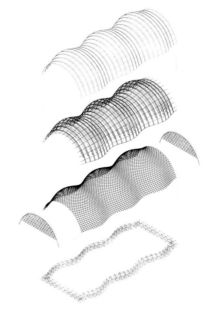

RIGHT **axonometric of construction system and view of paper-tube structure**

ARCHITECT
**Peter Testa Architects
(with Hans-Michael
Foeldeak, Ian Ferguson,
Devyn Weiser) and
Jeffrey Tsui/MIT**

YEAR
2001–2002 (unbuilt)

STRUCTURAL & MECHANICAL
ENGINEER
ARUP Services Ltd.

In his book *Lightness,* the Dutch physicist Adriaan Beukers claimed that if materials were lighter, less energy would be spent constructing buildings, since all materials must be transported or lifted by machinery at one time or another, and fossil-fuel burning trucks, airplanes, and cranes would need less power to move the loads. Peter Testa and his students at the Massachusetts Institute of Technology put this idea into practice with the Carbon Skyscraper, which uses sinuous strands of resin-impregnated carbon fiber that are lighter and stronger than steel.

BUILDING TYPE
● high-rise

ENERGY GENERATION
● energy conservation systems

LIGHT & AIR
● daylight illumination
● natural ventilation systems
● operable windows

CONSTRUCTION
● modular construction
techniques

URBANISM
● mixed-use building

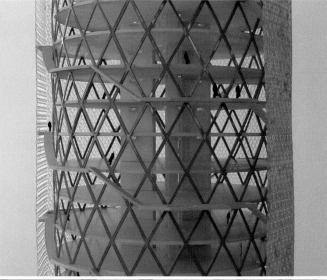

ABOVE **view of model,
Carbon Skyscraper,
Peter Testa Architects**

OPPOSITE **detail of model,
Carbon Skyscraper
version II, Jeffrey Tsui**

Rethinking the Corporate Biosphere:
The Social Ecology of Sustainable Architecture

by David Serlin

In 1998, the U.S.-based Building Owners and Managers Association gave the Enron Corporation the International Office Building of the Year Corporate Facility award. The prestigious honor recognized Enron's commitment to energy efficiency when, in the early 1990s, the corporation decided to upgrade the mechanical, lighting, and climate-control systems in its downtown Houston office building. In addition to using low-wattage fluorescent lights and running two massive generators at half speed rather than one at full speed, the Enron Building featured an automation system that regulated the entire structure's energy use. According to Stephen B. Woods, the corporation's director of facilities operation, Enron's was the first building in Houston to be recognized as a Green Lights partner, a distinction that carried enormous architectural and political symbolism for one of the largest energy brokers in the United States. In 2000, the Environmental Protection Agency awarded the Enron Building its Energy Star label, an honor given to a small number of corporate skyscrapers in the United States — perhaps a hundred or so — that boast efficient use of energy as well as reduction of harmful emissions. At the height of its powers, in 1999, Enron broke ground on an adjacent plot of land to build a 40-story, 1.2 million-square-foot office tower. Designed by Cesar Pelli & Associates, the new Enron Building promised similar or even greater use of environmentally conscious materials and technologies when it opened in the fall of 2001.[1]

Enron building, Houston Texas

1. See Gene Church Schulz, "Enron Building's Efficiency Earns an Energy Star," June 5, 2000, at www.archnews.com.

Enron's commitment to green transformations of the modern office building might have been its greatest legacy if its name hadn't become synonymous with one of the most controversial cases of bankruptcy in U.S. business history. In light of the revelations about the company's organizational problems, Enron's contribution to the sustainable architecture movement might seem a marginal or unrelated aspect of its history. Yet such an attitude obscures the valuable insights that can be gained from analyzing Enron from within the discourse of sustainability. Enron is one of many corporations that worked with good-faith efforts to create a cost- and energy-efficient work environment for the twenty-first century, yet with little concern or understanding for the nature of work or the ecology of the work experience. In the corporate world, the Enron Building and many other green office buildings provide examples of the success of architectural ecology at the expense of social ecology. One fears that sustainable design is in danger of becoming the manicured emerald-green Astroturf that covers the nutrient-depleted brown soil of problematic business practices.

Confronting the Enron debacle as a modern crisis of capitalism and design compels us to consider the multiple social and political dimensions of sustainability outside their immediate architectural context. This is especially true as more local governments, corporations, and private citizens in both Western and non-Western countries endorse sustainability programs in order to seek out practical solutions to centuries of environmental degradation and resource depletion as well as the manifest problems of urban planning and population density.

It is too facile and shortsighted to say that economic growth and architectural ecology are, by definition, antithetical, or that free-market economics is incompatible with sustainable building practices. Yet it is also important to point out that sustainable architecture does not in and of itself transform human relationships any more than sustainable buildings transform the business practices of corporations. If the only incentive for corporations to build sustainable skyscrapers is to win friends and influence shareholders, then sustainability as an architectural *and* social practice becomes muddied or turned into a sound bite. And if, as economic theorists insist, corporate growth and expansion are the prophets of modernization and democracy, then the buildings that sustain them should be flexible enough structurally to accommodate the multiple ecosystems that coexist on our planet.

For some, however, the green revolution in architectural design that began in the United States and Europe as a response to ecological issues such as resource depletion and global warming has been supplanted by a revolution not in sustainability itself but in the highly seductive concept of sustainability as a marketing tool. Some have derided this move toward sustainability as a fashionable exercise by multinational giants to boost their reputations as card-carrying players in the global green marketplace, what Helene Guldberg and Peter Sammonds have called "design tokenism."[2]

2. Helene Guldberg and Peter Sammonds, "Design Tokenism and Global Warming," in Abley and Heartfield, eds., *Sustaining Architecture in the Anti-Machine Age*, 72–84.

Indeed, many interpret a company's use of recycled office products as a public-relations device rather than a long-term ideological commitment to ecological values. As Catherine Slessor has argued, despite advances in green thought and design, "architects are still contriving to graft air-conditioned glass stumps on to city centres from Dallas to Dacca, and most inhabitants of the First World continue to pursue disparate work, shopping, and leisure activities by car."[3] Consequently, we continue, at our peril, to ignore the larger social goals addressed by the sustainability movement, which originated from heightened political consciousness as well as ecological awareness. Defanged of its political critique of excessive resource use and unbridled consumerism, the complex syntax of architectural sustainability is thus downgraded to the pidgin English of lifestyle choice and upscale marketing, the Body Shop–ization of contemporary environmental discourse.

In his design manifesto for sustainable buildings, *The Green Skyscraper*, architect and critic Kenneth Yeang asks one deceptively simple question: What kind of work gets done in a skyscraper?[4] Yeang does not mean literally what function does a skyscraper serve; instead, he poses the question philosophically to suggest that built environments, like their natural counterparts, are organic ecosystems that must work interdependently within existing social and political landscapes if all of the constituent parts are to thrive. Without a corresponding commitment to the social ecology of contemporary workplaces and the dynamics of human relationships in corporate settings, even the greenest of green buildings is only partially fulfilling the work it has set out to do. This is what makes the Enron Building a parody of sustainability rather than its champion: It urges us to ask what exactly makes a building an environmental success story if it gently hugs Mother Nature while eviscerating the livelihoods of its trusting employees.

Sustainable buildings present a practical alternative to the skyscraper's legacy of waste and excess by establishing the centrality of self-contained workplaces in the architectural ecology of modern cities. Work interiors and their attendant technologies are the spatial matrices through which humans interact with buildings and each another. For example, the modern elevator is one of the few socio-spatial environments designed by a collaboration of professionals as diverse as architects, acoustic engineers, and industrial psychologists. Despite recent innovations in elevator design, the practice of placing elevator shafts on a building's exterior walls, so as to expose a structure's normally hidden details, does nothing to challenge or transform the awkwardness of social interaction in cramped spaces, no matter how beautifully designed they are. Good technological design, like good sustainable buildings, should promote alternatives for spatial interaction. Good design should force its users to examine the rote memorization of social roles and express creativity in reframing or reinterpreting those roles within the parameters of the built environment.

We must consider a new configuration of the ecology of the work-

3. Catherine Slessor, *Eco-Tech: Sustainable Architecture and High Technology* (New York: Thames and Hudson, 1997), 12–13.

4. Kenneth Yeang, *The Green Skyscraper: The Basis for Designing Sustainable Intensive Buildings* (New York: Prestel, 1999).

place in order to understand how its interdependent social, political, and economic worlds are housed, nurtured, and sustained. Good design, for example, is often lauded for interrupting, or challenging, what sociologist Marcel Mauss calls our "habitus," that is, the regulated social behaviors that we perform daily, such as walking, to which we rarely give a second thought.[5] As the work of Frank Gehry, Philip Johnson, and I.M. Pei demonstrates, counterintuitive design can advance a traditionally conservative discipline like architecture. The unconscious, repetitive patterns of architectural habitus that plague Western skyscraper paradigms are precisely what the sustainable architecture movement seeks to confront and challenge. Why not extend such consciousness-raising to the social activities that go on within that architecture? If we can imagine the regular interactions of human beings as part of a fragile ecosystem within a larger system of architectural space, then interior spaces such as elevators, workstations, conference rooms, staff lounges, and even bathrooms should be seen as the internal viscera of the architectural organism.

Ideally, a sustainable building not only fulfills the architect's structural and ecological mandates but also honors a delicately balanced and interconnected set of human, architectural, and environmental subsystems. Isn't the whole point of green design to reconcile the demands of an artificial environment with a reverence for the natural materials and spaces in which humans thrive? The putative long-term goal of green skyscrapers, after all, is the survival of cities, their inhabitants, and the resources that sustain them. We might imagine the sustainable skyscraper as a kind of corporate biosphere, invoking the example of the Biosphere II project financed by the Bass family in the late 1980s and currently maintained by the Center for International Earth Science Information Network at Columbia University. As a combination energy station, research unit, educational facility, and living community, Biosphere II promotes a full-scale model of socio-ecological symbiosis that most green skyscrapers would do well to emulate. By thinking of sustainable buildings as dynamic terrariums attuned to their environments, architects and urban planners can promote the enduring environmental benefits as well as the enduring cultural legacies of what they create. Learning from the brutal example provided by Enron, we can build corporate biospheres in which all manner of flora and fauna thrive.

Recycling for Life

No other word communicates so effectively the concept of sustainability in the corporate world as "recycle"—or, rather, "recyclable," since the adjectival form contains so much less social pressure than the verb. Although recycling immediately calls to mind the familiar blue and green receptacles (which are themselves made from recycled plastics, and which typically hold recycled paper products printed with soy-based inks), it takes on a multiplicity of forms beyond the walls of the photocopy room. Biodegradable or

interior of Biosphere II

5. See Marcel Mauss, "Techniques of the Body," in Jonathan Crary and Sanford Kwinter, eds., *Incorporations* (New York: Zone, 1992).

easily recyclable products, renewable energy resources, and efficiently processed or reusable waste material are central to any sustainability program.

Using recycled paper products is, of course, one of the few practices of sustainability in which older buildings can participate, making it a mobile ecological strategy that does not require extensive structural planning or site-specific alteration. Recycling, however, also provides a model for understanding the possibilities of social interaction in a corporate culture committed to sustainability. The Post-It note, for example, may not seem like a green technology, let alone one that highlights the importance of renewable resources. In 1968, 3M scientist Spence Silver regarded his tricky adhesive as just another failed glue compound. It was subsequently applied to small, thin sheets of paper in order to produce temporary bookmarks, and in the late 1970s, 3M conducted a trial run of its new product, distributing it to secretaries who found a multitude of uses for the sticky sheets far beyond what the 3M designers expected. By the 1990s, the Post-It note had ascended to iconic status as one of the top-selling office supplies of the late twentieth century. Indeed, in 2001 curator Paola Antonelli included the humble Post-It as part of "Workspheres," the Museum of Modern Art's exhibition on good design in the contemporary office.

What remains vital and relevant about the Post-It note more than 20 years after its introduction is not its petrochemical pedigree. It is, in fact, one of the few office technologies that allows for a wide margin of creative flexibility. Unlike elevators or telephones or computer networks that require participants to obey the mechanical parameters of their social protocols, the small sticky yellow squares are nonhierarchical and open-ended, their vernacular meaning dictated by the subjective needs of the individual. They can be used and reused, written upon and erased, and combined, altered, rearranged, and discarded at any time without threatening the integrity of the workplace. In this sense, the Post-It note affirms the social ecology of the work environment by creating new contexts for sustaining interaction and creativity, promoting human intervention over structural constraints.[6]

In and of itself, of course, the Post-It note may not fit the formal definition of a sustainable technology. But its inherent adaptability and simplicity parallels that of an increasing number of technologies used in green skyscrapers that foreground the social and spatial relationships between humans and the built environment. Regenerative ventilation systems developed by firms such as ARUP Services Ltd. are an excellent case in point. Based on the principle that a building can be designed (some might say empowered) structurally to generate and recycle enough of its own energy to become self-sustaining, the ARUP system absorbs heat from human bodies, computer equipment, plants, and other heat-releasing sources within work-space interiors. This heat is captured, stored, and harnessed for later use. Although the increasing popularity of regenerative ventilation systems is rooted in their cost effective-

OPPOSITE LEFT **Personal Environment air system, Johnson Controls, Inc.** OPPOSITE RIGHT **diagram of air system in Helicon, London, England, Sheppard Robson, 1996**

6. For more about structural constraints, see Donald Norman, *The Design of Everyday Things* (New York: Doubleday, 1990).

ness and energy efficiency, the social ecology of the workplace also benefits significantly.

Regenerative systems are distantly related to energy-efficient technology such as the Personal Environment, designed in the mid-1990s by climate engineers at Johnson Controls and currently in production. The Personal Environment is an individualized air-conditioning, filtration, and environmental lighting device that can be used to combat the exorbitant costs of heating or cooling an entire building. Two small cooling and filtration units and one large flat heating panel at foot-level—cast in unobtrusive white molded plastic—are connected beneath a desk by thick gray plastic tubing that runs to a central air shaft. The office worker can regulate his or her own immediate workspace without being at the mercy of the building's thermostat, and the workstation becomes the spatial equivalent of a private weather envelope: It can be as light or as dark as the office worker wants it to be, as cold as a meat locker or as temperate as San Diego in September.

While the Personal Environment shares the regenerative ventilation model's mandate to use energy wisely and efficiently, regenerative systems represent a much different degree of collective investment. In a regenerative system, human bodies and built environments are mutually dependent, in much the same way they are in igloos, where the heat generated by human bodies is integral to the way the building functions. This dual focus on architectural and social sustainability encourages, and even demands, that

individuals participate proactively in the technologies they use and the spaces they inhabit, especially if such collective action involves a shared responsibility in the services provided by the tenants of the building. In high-rise residential skyscrapers, applied versions of the regenerative ventilation system could transform typical tenant-landlord or cooperative board member relationships by providing civic and moral injunctions to collective activity and group involvement. Such participation could not only change the static nature of large, impersonal buildings but could keep internal structures from becoming rigidly determined by bureaucracy, habit, or ennui. In this sense, recycled energy systems—especially those that transform energy for myriad uses—provide an alternative to a sustainable architecture that merely puts a green face on expropriated labor.

The Value of Impermanence

In a post–September 11 world where the architectural and social reconstruction of urban areas are deeply intertwined, meaning flows as much from architecture's adaptability as it does from a technology's ecological design. Low-energy building forms such as molded plywood, poured concrete, or glass brick, and renewable materials such as biodegradable fibers might be understood themselves as assets that can be recycled, indicating the degree to which ecological sustainability emphasizes flexibility over permanence. Thinking about a material's impermanence is a conceptual leap that does not imply cowardice or vulnerability but instead the

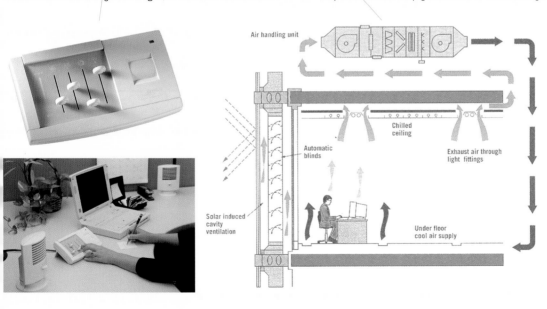

Air handling unit

Chilled ceiling

Automatic blinds

Exhaust air through light fittings

Solar induced cavity ventilation

Under floor cool air supply

strength and vitality that comes with being truly prepared for anything that might happen in an urban environment.

A low-tech version of this philosophy was seen recently in an unlikely and decidedly non-Western context. In the wake of U.S. military operations in the Middle East, thousands of citizens of Kabul, Afghanistan, have sought out ways to rebuild their cities by rummaging through the wreckage. Like their counterparts in Bosnia and Kosovo, Afghans were implored to consider the unexpected benefits of rubble rather than wait for new building materials that had the imprimatur of modernity. Bricks found in good condition, for example, are being used to refashion homes and schools, while debris is being used to rebuild roads, and scrap metal is being melted down for industrial and commercial uses. Wuria Karadaghy, who directs the rubble-recycling program for the United Nations, suggested that for Afghans, true sustainability demands that we not only rethink the materials we use but that we also temper the unrealistic expectations we have inspired among non-Western peoples for the gleaming spires of Western-style architecture. "[T]he Afghans thought we were going to rebuild their city for them, and put up aluminum and glass buildings. . . . This makes them realize that they are going to have to do it themselves, and that it will be done in accordance with their traditions."[7]

What expectations do we want to impart to future generations in accordance with our own architectural traditions? Clearly, the example of building materials as used by Afghan war survivors

defines the practice of recycling as one performed out of necessity rather than by choice. Yet Western architects and builders, even at their most privileged, still must recognize the desirable effects of using flexible materials that influence architectural form.

Collective Spaces and Sustainable Futures

Interiors that provide easy access to light and air may seem obvious in the vocabulary of sustainable architecture, but they also advance sustainability's often underserved mandate to break down hierarchical barriers between social groups such as administrators and employees, who historically have had different levels of access to natural elements. In William McDonough's design for Herman Miller's corporate headquarters in Holland, Michigan, for example, spaces for office work and light manufacturing are divided not vertically but horizontally by a sun-drenched "street" of enormous glass walls through which all employees must pass. Both groups have equal access to light and air, thereby diffusing social hierarchies associated with different kinds of work while simultaneously lowering energy costs. McDonough's design, which won the first annual *Business Week/Architectural Record* Good Design Is Good Business award, recognizes that even when economic incentives are the real motivation, the tools of sustainability can create a meaningful social effect. As the architect declared, the building "increased productivity at [Herman Miller] by 24 percent. At their volume, that increase is worth $60 million a year to Herman Miller. The building cost

RIGHT **main workroom, Larkin Building, Buffalo, New York, Frank Lloyd Wright, 1906**

OPPOSITE LEFT **employee swimming pool, Century Tower, Tokyo, Japan, Foster and Partners, 1991**

OPPOSITE RIGHT **European Court of Human Rights, Strasbourg, France, Richard Rogers Partnership, 1995**

7. Karadaghy, quoted in Dexter Filkins, "Brick by Brick, Afghans Recycle and Rebuild City," *New York Times* (April 15, 2002), A20.

$15 million. Ask any CEO if he'd accept a 400 percent return on his investment. This isn't rocket science, you know."[8]

If architects and clients acknowledged more explicitly how the success or failure of a particular engineered building is deeply implicated in the well-being of the social organism, both corporate entities and the general public might begin to appreciate more fully the architectural and social repercussions of sustainable buildings. Frank Lloyd Wright's Larkin Administration Building, for example, built in Buffalo, New York, in 1906, is considered the first modern office space. But its status in architectural history was assured the moment that Wright took into account the effect of a healthy work environment on the physical and psychological development of the company's employees. The main administration area in the Larkin Building was designed, with Wright's typical angular austerity, as an immense work space of natural woods and muted earth tones flooded with natural sunlight.

Wright's focus on the salutary effects of architectural space remains a standard for architects committed to sustainability as both an economic and social philosophy. In Tokyo's Century Tower, for example, Norman Foster's first building in Japan, the architect makes a nod to Wright's philosophy, addressing the organizational emphasis on the health and well-being of corporate employees and referencing traditional Japanese aesthetics of space and light. The Century Tower actually comprises two separate office buildings conjoined by a 19-story atrium (the tallest interior space of its kind in Japan when it was built in 1991), which admits sunlight from every conceivable angle. A separate facility attached to the structure offers staff amenities including a cafeteria and swimming pool. The swimming pool sits beneath an enormous, barrel-shaped convex roof, through which sunlight filters. An adjacent opaque glass divider allows staff members on duty to see both the light and the water. Unlike facilities in other skyscrapers that are designed in below-ground or leftover spaces, Foster's is a highly aestheticized environment that complements the skyscraper.

Architects like McDonough and Foster design buildings not merely for the purpose of creating monumentality or spectacle but to elevate basic human social needs within the context of otherwise utilitarian architecture. Just as ecological and social needs should exist in some type of dialectical relationship, sustainable buildings should use spatial adaptability to encourage a wide variety of activities. The European Court of Human Rights in Strasbourg, France, designed by Richard Rogers in 1995, is a beautiful example of a building whose austere administrative and legal status is quite literally diffused by light-capturing windows and an architectural morphology that resembles the physical structure of an insect. The seemingly awkward circular interior spaces, faced in steel, concrete, and energy-absorbing glass, are intentionally designed with a commitment to public access. The organic shape allows for natural ventilation, which, combined with the building's concrete foundation and its proximity to the banks of the River Ill, allows the court to

8. McDonough, quoted in Ken Shulman, "Think Green," *Metropolis* (August/September 2001), 80.

151

avoid massive air-conditioning bills in the summer. The dual commitment to architectural and social sustainability mirrors the court's commitment to preserving and defending human rights, an especially thorny project given the national and ethnic complexities of the post—Cold War era. The entrance plaza, entrance hall, and spaces for administration and adjudication are meant, as Catherine Slessor has observed, to demystify rather than obscure the inner workings of international human-rights law.[9]

In this sense, one might think of sustainability—as both a social and ecological mandate—as the architectural adjunct to the universal design movement, popular in Europe since the 1980s but only now beginning to develop roots in the United States. Universal designers work to create a nonhierarchical vocabulary for interior spaces and consumer products that can be used not only by populations with limited access (such as the disabled and elderly) but by all people regardless of ability or body type. Successful examples of universal design include kitchen appliances, such as large-grip vegetable peelers, and doors that can be opened without great strength or physical coordination. These objects can neutralize the stigma that often comes with designs for special-needs groups. If universal designers can make objects like vegetable peelers responsive to all needs and productive for all users, architects can design buildings like the European Court of Human Rights to be architecturally responsible as well as socially productive.

Of course, there's a big difference between civic buildings and commercial projects. The political function of civic buildings in the social ecology of cities and nations is understood as a precondition, rather than an aftereffect, of their existence. How, then, can we understand the political function of office buildings, especially as architecturally responsible and socially productive in the life of the city and the nation? The political function of sustainable skyscrapers is even more complex, since they have a competing set of hierarchical and social barriers with which to contend. Typically, skyscrapers in urban environments alienate—and, in some cases, displace—local populations that sustain the residential and commercial uses of the local landscape. In densely populated urban environments, the reach of these corporate biospheres extends far beyond the immediate proximity of the urban spaces they occupy. One way to ensure that architecture is a part of the social ecology of the city is to follow universal design's example and put the needs of the human body—in all its multifarious and vulnerable dimensions—at the heart of sustainability's social philosophy.

Norman Foster's skyscraper design for Swiss Re, a multinational reinsurance company, offers a brilliant antidote to the problem of achieving architectural sustainability at the expense of social sustainability. The Swiss Re Building self-consciously incorporates green spaces for both employees and the public, providing a beacon of hope for people who have come to regard large-scale building projects with skepticism. This is the only imaginable future for urban spaces—one that takes into account not only the building's

Swiss Re Headquarters, London, Foster and Partners, 1997–2004

9. Slessor, 178–83.

staff but the multiple populations that the neighborhood serves.

Conclusion

During the City Beautiful and Progressive reform movements of the late nineteenth and early twentieth centuries, local governments and philanthropists commissioned architects to construct stately, monumental buildings that appeared impervious to decay or change. Despite the magnificence of these structures and their materials, they represented the demands of an increasingly global capitalism for passive armies of workers who would regard these public spaces with civic pride and patriotism, thereby reinforcing the social order.[10]

In the twenty-first century, the social ecology in which we live depends on how well architects and urban planners make choices for buildings and communities that will endure not through solidity but through flexibility. Unlike previous generations' skyscrapers, whose reputations relied on their status as impermeable cathedrals of commerce, green skyscrapers must be more ecumenical than ever before. They must follow sustainability's architectural *and* ethical mandates to put buildings at the service of ecological safety and social accountability. The need for true participatory democracy has never been more urgent, and sustainable skyscrapers—as centers of financial and civic importance—can serve as champions of a new world order in which architecture is a social instrument of public good. This is especially true as we come to understand that the binary terms through which we have historically viewed the world—Western versus non-Western, urban versus suburban, developing versus postindustrial—are ecological and political remnants of an era when sustainability as an architectural practice in the West was either nonexistent or considered optional. Green skyscrapers have made us see that unhealthy buildings are costly, inefficient, and toxic on an architectural scale. Now we need to consider how the social limitations produced by both healthy and unhealthy buildings are costly, inefficient, and toxic on a human scale. As Paul Hyett has argued, "If sustainable design isn't a moral imperative, what is?"[11]

David Serlin is a research historian on the history of medicine at the National Institutes of Health and teaches American history in New York City.

Grand Central Station, New York City, Reed and Stem; Warren and Wetmore, 1903–1913

10. For historical and critical accounts of the City Beautiful movement as a form of social control, see M. Christine Boyer, *Dreaming the Rational City: The Myth of American City Planning* (Cambridge: MIT Press, 1983) and Elizabeth Wilson, *The Sphinx in the City: Urban Life, the Control of Disorder, and Women* (Berkeley: University of California Press, 1992).

11. Paul Hyett, "If Sustainable Design Isn't a Moral Imperative, What Is?" in Abley and Heartfield, eds., *Sustaining Architecture in the Anti-Machine Age* (Chichester, England: Wiley-Academic, 2001), 22–31.

153

URBANISM

There is no one formula for a mix of culture and technology that makes cities vibrant and livable. However, building regulations that promote environmentally sensitive development are finally beginning to appear in American cities. One notable example: the sustainable development codes written by Fox & Fowle Architects and the Battery Park City Authority for Battery Park City in New York, which regulate energy conservation, air quality, water conservation, and material use, and promote pedestrian activity and public transit use. From an environmental perspective, few if any Western cities are ideally planned, but this vital, recovering neighborhood may lead the way for responsible development in the future.

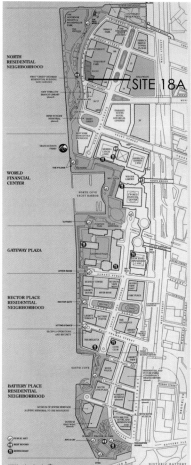

ABOVE **Battery Park City site plan**

TOP **montage of project in Battery Park City**

ABOVE **site model**

44. PROJECT
20 River Terrace

This 252-unit apartment building is the first to be designed under an ambitious set of new guidelines developed by the Battery Park City Authority and modeled on the LEED rating system, and it will be the first green high-rise residential building in the United States. The design incorporates photovoltaics, a geothermal system, black-water treatment for the reuse of water in toilets and irrigation of a neighboring park, gas-absorption chillers, and occupancy sensor systems for lighting and climate control. A detailed analysis of the exterior wall system components and construction methods completed by Steven Winter Associates during the design phase helped make the building 38 percent more energy efficient than required by New York State energy codes.

DESIGN ARCHITECT
Cesar Pelli & Associates

ARCHITECT OF RECORD
Schuman, Lichtenstein, Claman, Efron

LOCATION
New York City

YEAR
2000–

CLIENT
Albanese Development Corporation

MECHANICAL, ENGINEERING & PLUMBING CONSULTANT
Flack & Kurtz, Inc.

STRUCTURAL CONSULTANT
Desimone, Chaplin, and Dobryn

GENERAL CONTRACTOR
Turner Construction Company

BUILDING TYPE
• high-rise

ENERGY GENERATION
• renewable energy use
• energy conservation systems

LIGHT & AIR
• daylight illumination
• operable windows

GREENERY, WASTE & WATER
• exterior gardens
• water conservation and reuse

URBANISM
• environmental planning
• public transportation access
• mixed-use building
• site reuse

ABOVE **computer rendering of project with other future buildings**

BELOW **roof garden concept**

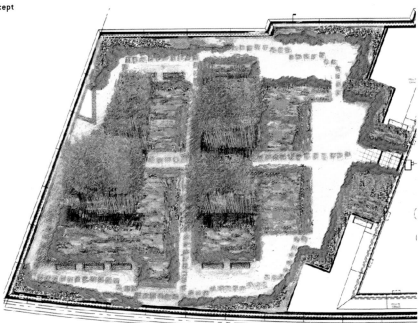

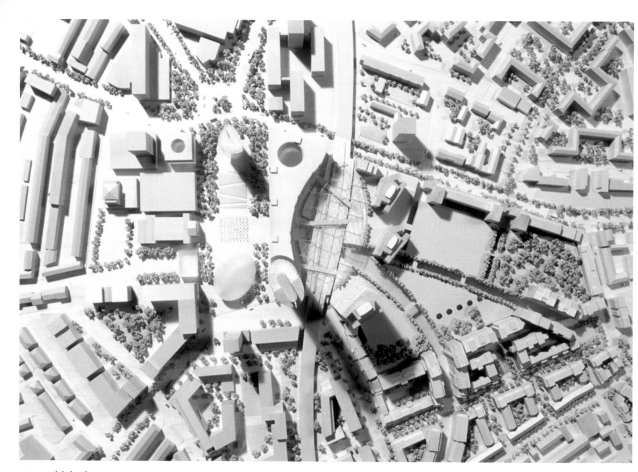

45. PROJECT
Elephant and Castle Master Plan

The plan to restructure this 200-acre southeast London neighborhood is the largest urban redevelopment project in the city. The area is a transport and traffic hub, with numerous above- and below-ground train lines and bus routes, and roads radiating toward eight of London's bridges. The master plan proposes radical changes based on environmental criteria: It restores public space to the community and banishes traffic from the site. In place of the existing central shopping area, the architects propose an enormous piazza—the largest public square in London—surrounded by trees, cafes, shops, housing, a sunken amphitheater, and a community arts center.

ARCHITECT
Foster and Partners

LOCATION
London, England

YEAR
2000–

CLIENT
Southwark Land Regeneration

ENGINEER
Battle McCarthy Consulting Engineers & Landscape Architects

CONTRACTOR
Gardiner and Theobald

BUILDING TYPE
- high-rise
- mid-rise
- long-span

ENERGY GENERATION
- renewable energy use
- energy conservation systems

LIGHT & AIR
- daylight illumination
- natural ventilation systems

GREENERY, WATER & WASTE
- interior and exterior gardens

URBANISM
- environmental planning
- public transportation access
- mixed-use building

LEFT **model showing mixed-use towers**

ABOVE **computer rendering of pedestrian, train, and underground circulation area**

ABOVE **view of buildings from storm water management pond**

46.

PROJECT
Gannett/USA TODAY Corporate Headquarters

The new Gannett/*USA TODAY* Corporate Headquarters is located near a major highway in the suburban woods. The dense grouping of buildings sets a new standard for responsible development, marking a shift away from sprawling suburban office parks. Two towers—one used by the Gannett Corporation and the other by *USA TODAY*—share a common base covered with greenery and terraced landscaping that absorbs run-off rainwater, minimizing soil erosion. A storm water management pond with an aerating fountain, a sediment trap, and biofiltration (through the cattails planted on its sides) reduces the project's impact on its surroundings.

ARCHITECT
Kohn Pedersen Fox Associates

INTERIOR ARCHITECT
Lehman-Smith + McLeish, P.L.L.C.

LOCATION
McLean, Virginia

YEAR
2001

CLIENT
Gannett Co., Inc./USA Today

LANDSCAPE ARCHITECT
Michael Vergason Landscape Architects

STRUCTURAL ENGINEER
CBM Architect

MECHANICAL, ELECTRICAL & PLUMBING ENGINEER
TOLK, Inc.

DEVELOPMENT MANAGER
Hines

GENERAL CONTRACTOR
The Clark Construction Group

BUILDING TYPE
● high-rise
● mid-rise

ENERGY GENERATION
● energy conservation systems

LIGHT & AIR
● daylight illumination
● natural ventilation systems
● monitored air quality

GREENERY, WATER & WASTE
● exterior gardens
● water conservation and reuse

URBANISM
● environmental planning

ABOVE **surrounding landscape and view of buildings from road**
LEFT **site plan showing relationship of building mass to surrounding landscape**
BOTTOM **view of buildings from road and terraced gardens**

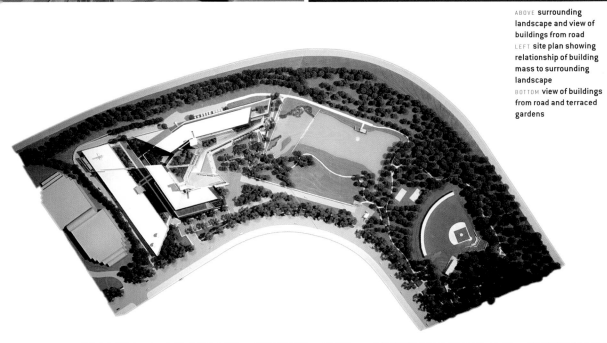

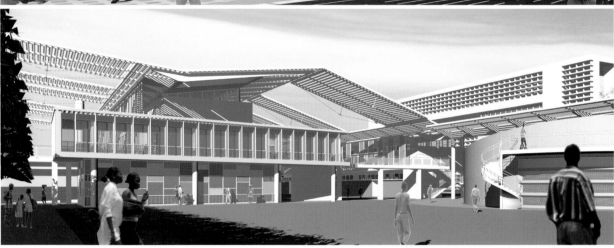

47.

PROJECT
Universidade Agostino Neto

Located on the southern edge of the city of Luanda, Angola, the Universidade Agostino Neto will accommodate 17,000 students. The campus will include chemistry, mathematics, physics, and computer science buildings, a central library, a rectory, and a conference center, as well as housing for students and faculty. A road surrounding the project marks a clear distinction between the inner ring, where the campus will be built, and the outer ring, where the natural landscape will remain untouched. The buildings are oriented to take advantage of natural light and the prevailing southwesterly winds. Classrooms and laboratories are organized in a linear sequence to maximize natural light. A single, undulating roof covers most of the campus and provides shading, as well as capturing wind and funneling it through the classrooms.

ARCHITECT
Ralph Johnson with Perkins & Will

LOCATION
Luanda, Angola

YEAR
2001–

CLIENT
Universidade Agostino Neto

STRUCTURAL & MECHANICAL ENGINEER
Dar Al-Handasah Consultants

ENVIRONMENTAL ENGINEER
Battle McCarthy Consulting Engineers & Landscape Architects

BUILDING TYPE
- low-rise
- mid-rise
- long-span

LIGHT & AIR
- daylight illumination
- natural ventilation systems
- operable windows

GREENERY, WATER & WASTE
- interior and exterior gardens
- water conservation and reuse

CONSTRUCTION
- use of renewable materials
- use of local or regional materials
- modular construction techniques

URBANISM
- environmental planning
- mixed-use building

ABOVE **computer rendering**
of administrative building
and sunken gardens

RIGHT **site plan**

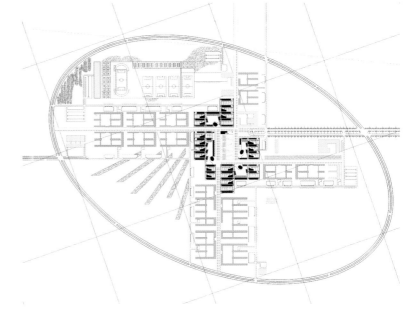

ARCHITECT
Richard Rogers
Partnership

LOCATION
Pu-Dong, Shanghai,
China

YEAR
1992–1994 (unbuilt)

CLIENT
Shanghai Municipality,
Pu-Dong New Area
Administration

ENVIRONMENTAL ENGINEER
ARUP Services Ltd.

In the Shanghai Master Plan, Richard Rogers Partnership explored the concept of a sustainable compact city for a community-based society. Public transportation, which encourages face-to-face contact and a more engaged local culture, is central to this proposal for a diverse commercial and residential quarter enhanced by a network of green parks and public plazas. At the heart of the project is a central park surrounded by a ring of low buildings. From this park, radiating boulevards connect six neighborhoods of 80,000 people each. The plan helps reduce automobile traffic and dependence on air-conditioning with pedestrian routes, greenery, and careful scaling of buildings.

BUILDING TYPE
- high-rise
- mid-rise

ENERGY GENERATION
- renewable energy use
- energy exporting
- energy conservation systems

LIGHT & AIR
- daylight illumination
- natural ventilation systems
- operable windows

GREENERY, WATER & WASTE
- interior and exterior gardens
- water conservation and reuse

CONSTRUCTION
- use of local or regional materials
- modular construction techniques

URBANISM
- environmental planning
- public transportation access
- mixed-use building
- site reuse

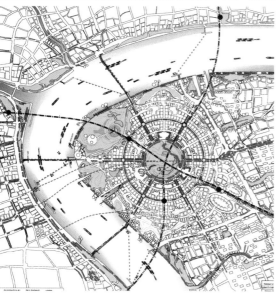

ABOVE **view of existing site**

ABOVE **diagram of roads and detail of marina model**

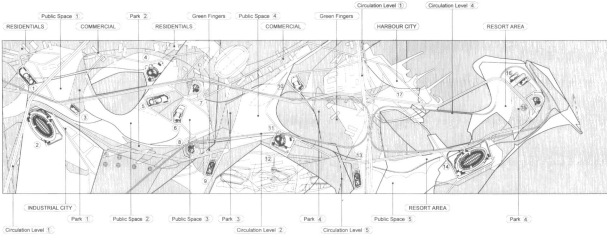

				Circulation Level ①	Circulation Level ④	
Public Space ①	Park ②	Green Fingers	Public Space ④	Green Fingers		
RESIDENTIALS	COMMERCIAL	RESIDENTIALS	COMMERCIAL		HARBOUR CITY	RESORT AREA

INDUSTRIAL CITY
Park ①   Public Space ②   Public Space ③   Park ③   Park ④   Public Space ⑤   RESORT AREA   Park ④
Circulation Level ①   Circulation Level ②   Circulation Level ⑤

TOP **view of model**   ABOVE **site plan**

49.

PROJECT
Eco-Tech City Master Plan

ARCHITECT
T.R. Hamzah and Yeang,
Snd. Bhd.

LOCATION
Rostock, Germany

YEAR
1997 (unbuilt)

Designed for an exhibition of planning concepts, Eco-Tech City is a master plan for a hypothetical community in Rostock, Germany. Towers based on the Menara Mesiniaga building and other prototypes are dispersed throughout a larger transportation and park network. The intention was to show the kind of urban form that could result from the use of high-rise towers in combination with extensively landscaped parks. The Eco-Tech City is connected by pedestrian routes, a light rail transit system, and automated people-movers.

BUILDING TYPE
● high-rise
● mid-rise

ENERGY GENERATION
● renewable energy use
● energy conservation systems

LIGHT & AIR
● daylight illumination
● operable windows

GREENERY, WATER & WASTE
● interior and exterior gardens
● water conservation and reuse

URBANISM
● environmental planning
● mixed-use building

ABOVE **towers from above
and view of towers in park**

ABOVE **view of model from above**

OPPOSITE **views of model showing distribution of towers in landscape**

50. PROJECT
Business and Advanced Technology Center (BATC)

The BATC campus includes a management center, a school for technological educational programs, research and development laboratories, convention and exposition centers, and student residences. What is unusual about the plan is the use of skyscrapers for university programs that are usually housed in low-rise buildings. The architects believe that the dense plan will reduce transportation costs and slow down the rapid development of the Malaysian countryside.

ARCHITECT
T.R. Hamzah and Yeang, Snd. Bhd.

LOCATION
Semarak, Malaysia

YEAR
1998–

CLIENT
Universiti Teknologi Malaysia

STRUCTURAL & MECHANICAL ENGINEER
Battle McCarthy Consulting Engineers & Landscape Architects

ENVIRONMENTAL ENGINEER
Juru Ukur Bahan

BUILDING TYPE
- high-rise
- mid-rise

ENERGY GENERATION
- renewable energy use
- energy conservation systems

LIGHT & AIR
- daylight illumination
- operable windows

GREENERY, WATER & WASTE
- interior and exterior gardens
- water conservation and reuse

URBANISM
- environmental planning
- mixed-use building

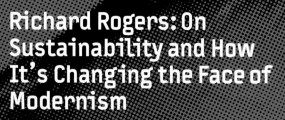

Richard Rogers: On Sustainability and How It's Changing the Face of Modernism

by Nina Rappaport

To get the practitioner's perspective, Nina Rappaport
interviewed several of the leading innovators in the field
of green design. Richard Rogers, the architect of Lloyd's of
London, is one of sustainability's best known proponents.
Chief advisor to the Mayor of London on architecture
and urbanism, he is the author of two seminal works on
sustainable cities, *Cities for a Small Planet* and *Cities for
a Small Country*. Here he discusses the history of the
sustainability movement and its new focus on large-
scale buildings and urban design.

Nina Rappaport, editor of Constructs *and other publications for Yale University, teaches at the Yale School of Architecture and the City College School of Architecture at the City University of New York.*

When did you first begin to address sustainability issues?

Environmental issues, including energy efficiency, have always figured in my work. I read Rachel Carson's *Silent Spring* shortly after its publication in 1962, and Buckminster Fuller's perspective on environmental issues has been immensely important for me. I became convinced that buildings needed to be flexible and adaptable, constructed for a long life and able to respond to society's changing requirements. Sustainable development implies an approach to the use and management of natural resources — doing more with less. The urgent task is to forge an environmentally responsible architecture . . . to use technology to achieve beneficial ends.

Your studies at Yale — where you looked at the work of architects such as Paul Rudolph, Rudolph Schindler, Buckminster Fuller, and the architects of the Case Study houses in California — clearly influenced your own design work. Who was the biggest influence?

The rational, machine-made aesthetic of the Case Study houses made an immense impression on me: My thesis at Yale was on Schindler and Soriano. Koenig, Ellwood, Soriano, and Charles and Ray Eames all championed practical, fast-track construction and the environmental advantages of prefabrication and mass-made industrial components. I fell in love with the idea of a mass-produced house and the potential of lightweight steel construction. In terms of influences, the daddy of sustainable architecture has to be Bucky Fuller, with his talk about Spaceship Earth, his Dynamaxion House of 1927 — which responded to the air and wind — and the huge importance he placed on resource efficiency. Fuller, in particular, saw the opportunity for a dramatic, design-liberating discipline for buildings, and that's something that has remained central to my own work.

The 1973 oil crisis made it obvious to most people that supplies of fossil fuel are not infinite. Did that have an immediate effect on building design?

Of course. In its way, the Pompidou Center was already at the cutting edge of efficient technology — very energy efficient by the terms of the early 1970s. The RIBA [Royal Institute of British Architects] was also on the case, with its "long life, loose fit, low energy" campaign. In fact, Pompidou was conceived before the movement to reduce energy consumption had gathered real momentum, but the building's inherent flexibility, social impact, and function as a catalyst for urban regeneration all proclaimed its sustainable credentials. Our first important assay at energy-saving design was the Zip-Up house of 1967 — a flexible, mass-produced, and highly insulated concept, a direct response to the need for instant, affordable, and adaptable housing. Low construction and running costs were the key issues. The house was heated by a two-kilowatt electric fire driven by a wind generator, and used a mass-produced cladding system with neoprene-fastening zips, allowing rapid assembly. The joy of the design was a completely flexible interior and adjustable legs — it could be reconfigured and sited anywhere.

In the past, you've said that sustainable buildings have their own aesthetic order. Is that still true in your work today?

Yes — the Law Courts Building we designed in Bordeaux in 1998 is a case in point. To counteract the traffic noise and pollution, we designed a highly layered building. The atrium acts as a buffer, providing a stable reservoir of clean, tempered air drawn through a waterfall, which cools and humidifies it. Supply air is drawn from the atrium into the offices through hollow ribs in the floor structure, which makes maximum use of the thermal mass of the

"When we we built the Daimler Chrysler headquarters in Berlin, the chairman told his workers, 'In the summer, you will take your jackets off when you are too hot, and in the winter, you will put on a pullover.' That probably does more for energy-efficiency than anything else. We don't think twice about [doing] this in our houses."

concrete and provides summer nighttime cooling. The distinctive organic form of the seven courtrooms was no whim—it was governed by the need to extract stale air through the upper extremity of the pods where they protrude above the undulating copper roof. It's a highly sustainable building that uses both traditional and innovative technology. I don't believe eco-building should be didactic. It should respond to a series of internal and external forces.

Do you see your eco-buildings as functioning machines that fulfill those goals?

Yes, they are big machines in one sense. But they have to serve people first and foremost. The program, the functional elements, and the construction elements of a building don't make architecture; it is imagination that makes architecture. The program is just the first building block. Structure, in itself, doesn't make a building: It is the use of imagination applied to structure, with sustainability as the driving force, that makes the building.

How is green architecture changing today?

Ecology-conscious buildings will change modern architecture more radically than perhaps any movement we have seen since the beginning of the modern movement. The problem is that there are powerful forces, especially in the United States, trying to strip eco-building of any real value. Where energy is unbelievably cheap, issues of pollution are of little interest. And big corporations come along with a full air-conditioned pack to fit into your office buildings. Whether you need it or not is irrelevant. It's like gas-guzzling cars—you don't drive them very fast, but everyone is used to them. You will see the disappearance of gas-guzzling cars and then that will affect the movement systems—

the streets, spaces, and buildings. We will see a tremendous revolution in the next 20 to 25 years. I hope we will recognize the need to reconsider buildings as well. It's not difficult.

Your work on master plans for sustainable cities is well known. Surely, designing one or two green buildings in a city is something of a token gesture? How can sustainability function on an urban scale if we have made so many mistakes already? Do you advocate creating policies to require that older buildings be retrofitted?

The oldest masonry buildings work much better, really. They mediate between inside and outside, cool off at night, and then keep the cool inside during the day. The most difficult structures are average office buildings—thin-skinned, sealed buildings—and we are lucky that they have very short lives and can be pulled down. Their only purpose was to make a quick buck—they have no value over a longer period. Now in Europe there are more building regulations that require energy efficiency. The price of gas rises all the time, and many European cities are starting to limit the amount of traffic they will allow. When we built the DaimlerChrysler Headquarters in Berlin, we said to them, "If you really want the building to be energy efficient, you have to incorporate a lot more energy conservation than the international code demands, which says that you have to be at 20°C all the time, and if you are one degree above or below you might get sued." The chairman of DaimlerChrysler told his workers, "In the summer, you will take your jackets off when you are too hot, and in the winter, you will put on a pullover." Now that probably does more for energy efficiency than anything else. We don't think twice about [doing] this in our houses. So we need to see a cultural change. We need to charge the real price of energy rather than subsidize it. You have to build a consensus.

How do you build a consensus in the United States, if eco-architecture is not a priority with architects?

By talking and exchanging ideas. As architects, we are always responding to needs that will affect form. There is a growing reaction to the change in weather patterns. We are beginning to realize the obligation to restore an ecological balance. Just as doctors adopt new medicines to cure people, so we have to cure the environment.

You've done master plan exercises for cities such as Shanghai and Berlin. How do you go about creating a sustainable city?

One of the best ways to achieve sustainability in a large-scale planning project is to spread energy use over a 24-hour period. An office building and a hotel could share an energy source, since one uses energy predominantly during the day and the other at night. Similarly, instead of relying on power stations, we could employ local systems, which would be much more efficient because so much energy is lost between the power creator and the point of dispersal. So you could have living, working, and leisure combined in a cohesive whole rather than the ghastly ghetto-like patterns that characterize so much of contemporary urban planning.

How can we make building construction practices more sustainable?

The running of a building is where a vast amount of energy consumption occurs. But having said that, you also have to think about construction materials. You can use timber, which is highly sustainable and easily replaceable, as long as it is not teak or a hardwood. And you can begin to look at materials you can recycle. None of our buildings uses straight air-conditioning— the air-conditioned box is basically dead.

What is your office currently working on?

We are doing research on the compact, mixed-use, well connected, and well designed eco-community and the relationship between public transportation and density. By comparing buildings that have low construction costs and high running costs with those that have low running costs, we can feed this information to the government for taxation purposes. We're doing political, technological, and economic work. We're the only architectural practice that does all of this.

Are you still optimistic about the environment?

I'm a born optimist—as long as we recognize that there are problems that we have to get over. It would be good to imagine that we don't have to experience a major crisis in order to take some action. As a civil society we have to be conscious of what is needed not just to maximize profit but to maximize value. And we *are* becoming more conscious of that—so yes, I am optimistic. If we can fuse social concerns, technological and structural innovation, and environmentally responsible design, I believe we can create architecture that properly reflects the requirements of the twenty-first century. ✿

Kenneth Yeang: Building Cities in the Sky

by Nina Rappaport

Kenneth Yeang, the author of numerous books including
The Skyscraper: Bioclimatically Considered,
The Green Skyscraper, and *A Vertical Theory of Urban
Design*, is widely known for his groundbreaking work
in large-scale sustainable design. He talks to Nina
Rappaport about his newest projects and the future
of green architecture.

Some of your work bears a strong resemblance to experimental architecture developed in the 1950s and 1960s. How did architects such as the Japanese Metabolists or the British group Archigram influence you?

Charles Jencks says that I am biomorphic and often refers to me as a Metabolist. I am a friend of Kisho Kurokawa—who is a wonderful mentor—and I also know Arata Isozaki, both members of the early Japanese Metabolist group. I admire their ideas, but I don't find their design interpretations significantly ecological. Peter Cook, Ron Herron, David Green, and Dennis Crompton of the Archigram group were my teachers when I was at the AA [Architectural Association] in London [1962–1971]. Cook was my fifth-year master, and he is still one of my more important critics. But I have departed into another area of design with green architecture—although Peter also likes to put veggies in his buildings.

Are you conscious of trying to create an architectural effect— a particular green aesthetic—or are your building designs entirely dictated by bioclimatic concerns?

I *am* searching for an ecological aesthetic, but in the final analysis it's the building's systemic aspects that are most important. My current ideas are based on our work on biomimesis (designing or learning by imitating nature) and ecomimesis (designing using analogies of ecosystems and ecology). I'm working on designing buildings that function as urban ecosystems. In the 1990s, when I was seeking an aesthetic, my work was more high tech. But by 2000 it looked more organic and biological, and was less about high-tech structures and less Euclidian in form. In a recent project, we used what we call "eco-cells," where we slot cellular voids into the building to allow in daylight, rainwater, vegetation, and natural

ventilation. We vary the built form so that it is not a solid block, and the building is integrated with the ground.

Was that an aesthetic decision or was it a response to climatic constraints?

If you want to be rigorous about it, the climatic factors actually dictate certain optimal forms. In reality, you realize that you can't always have the ideal form because of the shape of the site, the neighbors, or the lack of sun to the building next door. There are no hard and fast rules. One goal is to maintain the continuity of the building with the landscape; the building should look as if it grows out of the landscape— not on the ground but of the ground. We see architecture as a prosthetic device, like an artificial arm. We want to integrate architecture with the organic host system. We also need to bring more organic mass into the city and bring in the biotic constituents. For the city we need to provide ecological corridors that tie all the green areas together. We can achieve this with landscape bridges and linkages of vegetation from the ground to the building.

This is where the influence of Ian McHarg's study Design with Nature *comes into your work. As he was looking at the natural environment, you are looking at the built.*

During my studies at the University of Pennsylvania, where I worked with Ian McHarg, I learned how every site is an ecosystem and that there is a limit to how much we can impose on it before irreparable damage is done. McHarg's use of the landscape layer-cake model for mapping was developed for ecological land-use planning in the 1960s. The planning preference is to ensure landscape continuity in the ecosystems and in the buildings.

If ecological or bioclimatic architecture is indeed dependent on the local climate, site, landscape, and wind, then shouldn't all ecological architecture look different? Or is there now a bioclimatic formula?

There is no bioclimatic formula. Early this year I conducted a workshop with students at the National University of Singapore to demonstrate that, even within this hot-humid climatic belt, buildings in three different locations — woodlands, coastal, city center — can have significant microclimatic differences and different architectures.

In Europe you have to deal with two extreme seasons — winter and summer — and then the two mid-seasons. So the energy systems and orientations for buildings in different locations have to be different. For example, London is 52 degrees latitude above the equator and the sun is very low, which means that the north facade of the building will not get much sun, so there is no point in putting any greenery there; we put the greenery on the south side of the building. So the sun path affects the shape of the building. In the tropics the shape of the building is different, because the sun path is different. We need first to optimize all passive-mode [bioclimatic] strategies before we proceed to mixed-mode systems, and then before using full-mode and productive-mode systems.

It is easier to use bioclimatic design in temperate climates, because in the mid-seasons we can use natural ventilation and still have a comfortable environment, whereas it is difficult in the tropics because of the high outside temperature and humidity.

Do you think it's ethical to build skyscrapers, even if they're green? Because of their sheer size and lack of context in so many non-Western cities, is it possible for skyscrapers to be truly responsive to site, culture, and climate?

I don't think skyscrapers should be built just anywhere — they should be built where they justify their existence by optimizing land use and reducing energy consumption through efficiency of transportation. But as cities grow there are few options to accommodate such growth, so I would intensify and optimize the city's land use. If you build high-rises, the preferred locations would be at transportation interchanges to reduce the use of cars and optimize the use of public transport. We also have to build them in as humane and environmentally friendly a way as we can.

Do you consider high-rise buildings to be urban design in and of themselves?

In a single building you can have something like 10 to 15 or more acres of built-up space, as in the World Trade Center. If you think of designing on 10 to 20 acres of land area, you would approach it as an urban design project, not just a building project. I have taken all the ideas about urban design — place making, landscaping, figure-ground relationships, accessibility — and asked, how do they work vertically? The objective is to recreate in the sky the pleasurable conditions that we find on the ground.

There should be different places in the sky for socializing. You would have not only a terrace, but also big secondary and tertiary parks, and amenities like the local pub, the stationery shop, and the chemist. They should not all be on the ground plane; they should be dispersed throughout the building.

"The problem with most architects is that when they get a project, they run off and start designing. We don't design until we have a detailed brief and have agreed on the budget ... [which] is usually based on an industry standard. This diffuses the debate about whether or not to have green features."

For the London local authority of Southwark we are placing parks in the sky in the high-rise and improving linkages in the urban ecosystem. On the ground plane you normally have many linkages and routes to get to a particular place, whereas in a skyscraper you have only a main elevator core and staircases. I believe skyscrapers should have more than just one circulation system, with secondary, tertiary, and even quaternary linkages sideways, such as bridges.

How do you convince clients to build green buildings? Do you have to talk them into it?

I have three types of clients: The first comes to me and wants a green building, so there is no problem. The second I get because I won the competition, and in that case they are obligated to build what I have designed. The third is the commercially driven client, which I am afraid represents 80 percent of my clientele. The problem with most architects is that when they get a project, they run off and start designing. In our case, we really don't design until we have a detailed brief and have agreed on the budget with the client. We then design to this budget. When we present a project, we say, "We met your budget requirements. Here are the costs to prove it." Then it is much easier to get the green aspects accepted. The budget is usually based on an industry standard for that building type. This diffuses the debate about whether or not to have the green features.

Do you think there should be a charter like the Charter of Athens or the United Nations Human Rights Charter to create goals for the future of green architecture, which all architects and building engineers could work toward?

We are actually working on one now, with the United Nations' environmental program. We have been invited with 60 people to develop a charter for city planning. Psychologists, economists, sociologists, politicians, and city planners have been invited to write something like the Ten Commandments of green building.

Which of your latest buildings is most successful at integrating engineering, design, ecological, and social issues?

The EDITT Tower in Singapore and our entry for the Kowloon waterfront competition are good examples. We just submitted a competition entry for a building in Amsterdam as our state-of-the-art building. We saw it in terms of flows—of energy, water, sewage, materials, vegetation, and people—that we tried to integrate into a single structure. An ecologist sees an ecosystem in terms of flows, and we are trying to look at buildings in the same way.

What is your goal with this latest project?

I want to continue to develop the idea of designing the urban ecosystem. There are still many technical problems that need to be solved. It is an agenda on which I hope to spend the rest of my life working. ⚙

Bruce Fowle, Robert Fox, and William Browning: It's Not Easy Building Green

by Nina Rappaport

Robert F. Fox, Jr., and Bruce S. Fowle, principals of Fox & Fowle Architects, and William D. Browning, senior associate of the Rocky Mountain Institute, collaborated on two of the most important recent green projects—the Condé Nast Building at Four Times Square and the Battery Park City Environmental Guidelines. Nina Rappaport talks to them about the difficulties of being environmentally sensitive on a large scale and why building consensus may be the biggest challenge in building green.

Fox & Fowle is known as a green architecture firm that came out of a fairly corporate architectural tradition. How did you build your first sustainable buildings in New York? Where did your research begin? And how did it all come together for a skyscraper like the Condé Nast Building at Four Times Square?

ROBERT FOX: The first major building we did in New York — 767 Third Avenue, designed in 1979 — was recently cited as a breakthrough in green design because it saved energy. Its ceiling diffuser would blow in as much air as required with an individually adjustable thermostat. We've been thinking about these issues for a while.

BRUCE FOWLE: It was key that the Durst family, who developed the Condé Nast Building, our greenest building to date, had a history of environmental awareness. Jody Durst uses a wood-burning stove to heat his house and cuts his own wood. Douglas Durst owns the largest organic farm in upstate New York. Since Jody and Douglas took over the family real estate business, they have been going through a process of greening their existing buildings. Dan Tishman, the construction manager on the project, has an organic farm in Maine, and his wife is a major player in the Audubon Society. My family is environmentally conscious, and at Fox & Fowle we have been pushing our projects toward sustainability when we've had the choice. It was the synergy and common interest of the three firms that really made Four Times Square work.

How did you manage to convince everyone to get on board with your ideas, and how was the collaboration on Four Times Square realized?

BRUCE FOWLE: As we were developing the project, we saw clearly that we were all thinking of a more environmentally correct approach. Shortly into the project, Sylvia Smith, a Fox &

Fowle principal, received a call from the Rocky Mountain Institute, which had initiated a new program to make sure design teams were adequately compensated to design environmentally responsible buildings. They asked if we would like our project be part of their program, and offered to help fund energy analysis services, including the DOE-2 computer analysis. We discussed the fact that green buildings in the U.S. to date were much smaller [than Four Times Square] — less than 50,000 square feet — and built for a single user who could create a statement. We quickly learned that no one knew all the answers about how to create a high-rise that was environmentally responsible. There was a big learning curve.

WILLIAM BROWNING: The Rocky Mountain Institute's Green Development Services (GDS) program provides research and consulting on environmental opportunities in the design and development of buildings and land. We have worked with such diverse clients as Wal-Mart, the White House, Disney, Shell, Hines, Lucasfilm, and the Pentagon. We were asked to meet with the Dursts and Fox & Fowle by a friend at United Technologies. The Four Times Square relationship was different from our normal consulting relationship: Four Times Square was one of four projects involved in a national experiment linking architectural and engineering fees to the measured level of energy efficiency a design achieves. The Performance-Based Fees experiment was funded by the Energy Foundation, and allowed GDS to coordinate energy design and computer modeling support for the design teams.

ROBERT FOX: When we started building Condé Nast, the real estate brokers wanted the typical standard of eight watts per square foot. So we designed it for eight watts, but subsequently did the Reuters headquarters at six watts per square foot. The 25 percent savings is an enormous amount of money on a $500 million building. In the future we hope to reduce the wattage even further by communicating to the tenants that they are really probably only using three watts. You can do this in any building, but you need to think about the mechanical system and not design the south side the same as the north side, and incorporate more individual controls.

What kinds of consultants did you bring in to work on the Condé Nast Building?

BRUCE FOWLE: We brought in specialists in photovoltaics and ice storage, Asher Durman on materials and embodied energy, Pamela Lippe, who runs Earth Day New York, for coordination, Steven Winter for detailed DOE-2 energy analysis, and Charles Eley for original DOE-2 analysis. And, of course, the project couldn't have happened without the dedication of the Dursts, who financed it.

Can high-rises ever really be considered green? Doesn't the construction alone consume too much energy?

WILLIAM BROWNING: Tall buildings do contain dense concentrations of material, and a large amount of energy is used to make those materials. However, over the life of a building, the embodied energy—the amount of energy it takes to make the materials and construct the building—is a small fraction of the energy consumed in operations. In a suburban setting, the individual cars commuting to and from a building can use a significant amount of energy as well. A tall, energy-efficient building in an urban setting where most workers use mass transit may be less energy-intensive than a low, large-floor-plate building in a suburban setting.

BRUCE FOWLE: A high-rise of 1.6 million square feet on 48 floors sits on one acre; if it were divided into individual structures in suburbia it would take up 140 acres, not including the required infrastructure for access and utilities. The incredible concentration on a small piece of land, which 95 percent of the workers— of whom there are 6,000—get to by public transportation in itself makes it sustainable. The single-roof surface of Four Times Square with all of its thermal exposure would be 48 times larger in a one-story building—a huge difference! Elevators, because they are counterweighted, are the most energy efficient means of transportation.

How did you convince the subcontractors to use environmentally sensitive building products?

BRUCE FOWLE: Dan Tishman's personal commitment was the most important factor, as he set the tone among the staff. There was a boilerplate in the specifications—subcontractors were forbidden to use volatile compounds or other materials and methods that would injure the health of their workers. We had a separate crew of mechanical engineers to evaluate the equipment and the way things were installed, and make sure that the controls were all working and that they were all calibrated. These checkups will continue to be done every five years.

ROBERT FOX: We also required the contractors to recycle the construction debris. They fought us because it was a lot of work, but then they realized that they could salvage the debris and make money. About 67 percent of the construction material was salvaged.

> "We required the contractors to recycle the construction debris. They fought us because it was a lot of work, but then they realized that they could salvage the debris and make money. About 67 percent of the construction material was salvaged."

How was the need for environmental guidelines established at Battery Park City?

ROBERT FOX: We developed an idea for the guidelines, and I went to the Battery Park City Authority and said, "If we could get a grant from NYSERDA [the New York State Energy Research Development Authority] to pay 50 percent and another sponsor to pay 25 percent, would you pay the last 25 percent, and we'll write guidelines for new residential buildings?" And we then received grants from Carrier and NYSERDA. We created a team with Flack & Kurtz, Asher Durman, the Rocky Mountain Institute, and the Natural Resources Defense Council. And because the guidelines were so successful, they hired us to adapt them for commercial buildings, which we just recently did.

How is a project in Battery Park now built within these guidelines? What process does an architect or developer follow?

BRUCE FOWLE: The Battery Park City Authority issues an RFP for a project where the owner-developer will pay for the lease of the land. The state has the ability to say, "We know that this first green residential building might cost $30 more per square foot, and we will absorb that in the differential of the bid—instead of X amount per year for land, we will get X minus Y." The guidelines don't say precisely how to design the buildings. They focus on overall goals, such as: You must reduce your energy consumption by a certain percent; five percent of your energy has to be from solar panels; you have to have a central air-conditioning system, not through-wall units; and interior spaces have to use nontoxic paint.

ROBERT FOX: From the work on these guidelines, we helped draft the New York State Green Building Tax Credit, which was passed. It was the first green tax credit in the country, and the organization that pushed it (besides the National Resources Defense Council) was the Real Estate Board of New York—a total surprise.

Are you currently working on other sustainable building projects?

BRUCE FOWLE: One Bryant Park—which we're designing for the Dursts—will have even more sophisticated systems [than Four Times Square]. The glass is more sophisticated, and the photovoltaics are more integral to the building design. We will also take another look at wind power on the roof. The air distribution will be under the floor to eliminate ductwork and to bring air in at a higher temperature and a lower speed, so you don't have energy loss, and you don't have to cool the entire height of the room by blowing the air down.

ROBERT FOX: We're also developing guidelines for the Second Avenue subway, where there are 16 different engineering disciplines—and all 16 have to be green. And we have written some guidelines for the New Jersey Transit Authority. We are trying to design buildings that people can learn from, such as a small office building for the Dodge Foundation. Since we started our Green Studio, people come to us to do green buildings and wonder why everyone isn't doing them.

Do you try to convince all your clients to build green buildings?

BRUCE FOWLE: We always raise the subject, and clients are always interested but skeptical because of the initial cost factors. But the owner-user likes the idea of a healthy environment, because if you can improve worker productivity through less absenteeism and greater motivation from natural daylight, then it makes a big difference financially. Clients don't have to go 100 percent green—any increment will help. Every step toward building sustainability is an achievement. ❂

Glossary of Terms Used in Sustainable Design

by Ashok Raiji

Ashok Raiji, a mechanical engineer and a principal at the engineering firm of ARUP Services Ltd., is a nationally recognized specialist in sustainable design and engineering.

a.

Active solar: A solar application that uses electrical or mechanical equipment (typically pumps or fans) to assist in collecting and storing solar energy for the purpose of heating or cooling (buildings, liquids, or gases) or to make electricity.

b.

Bakeout: A process used to remove VOCs in a building by operating the building's HVAC systems at elevated temperatures using 100 percent outside air after all the furniture and finishes (carpeting, ceiling tiles, etc.) have been installed.

Biomass: An energy resource derived from organic matter such as wood, agricultural waste, or other living cell material.

Bioremediation: The use of natural biological organisms (microbes, bacteria, plants, etc.) to break down contaminants and restore contaminated land to productive use.

Black water: Wastewater from toilets and urinals, which contains pathogens that must be neutralized before the water can be safely reused. After neutralization, black water is typically used for non-potable purposes, such as flushing or irrigation.

BREEAM: The Building Research Establishment Environmental Assessment Method (BREEAM) is a comprehensive tool for analyzing and improving the environmental performance of buildings through design and operations. This methodology has been developed by the U.K.-based Building Research Establishment. Additional information can be found at www.bre.co.uk.

Brownfield: An abandoned or underused site. Brownfields are often the site of old industrial complexes, gasoline stations, oil storage facilities, and other buildings that used chemicals that may have polluted soil and ground water. Regeneration of brownfields is a sustainable activity, since the process involves cleanup of a polluted site and consequent efficient land use.

Building envelope: Elements (walls, windows, roofs, skylights, etc.) and materials (insulation, vapor barriers, siding, etc.) that enclose a building. The building envelope is the thermal barrier between the indoor and outdoor environments and is a key factor in the sustainability of a building. A well-designed building envelope will minimize energy consumption for cooling and heating, and promote the influx of natural light.

c.

Carbon dioxide (CO_2): Carbon dioxide is a colorless, odorless gas that exists naturally in the Earth's atmosphere. The major source of man-made CO_2 emissions is the combustion of fossil fuels. Carbon dioxide is the primary greenhouse gas and is known to contribute to global warming and climate change. Atmospheric concentrations of CO_2 have been increasing at a rate of about 0.5 percent per year and are now approximately 30 percent above preindustrial levels.

Cogeneration: A process in which power is produced by a gas-fired engine and generator set. Heat produced in this way is used as heating and/or cooling media. A cogeneration plant is often referred to as a combined heat and power plant.

d.

Daylighting: The use of natural light to supplement or replace artificial lighting.

e.

Embodied energy: The total energy used to create a product, including the energy used in mining or harvesting, processing, fabricating, and transporting the product.

Energy efficiency: The ratio of energy output of a conversion process or a system to its energy input.

f.

Fly ash: The fine ash waste collected by flue gases from coal burning power plants, smelters, and waste incinerators. Fly ash can be used as a cement substitute in concrete, reducing the concrete's embodied energy.

Fossil fuels: Fuels found in the Earth's strata that are derived from the fossilized remains of animal and plant matter over millions of years. Fossil fuels include oil, natural gas, shale, and coal. Fossil fuels are considered nonrenewable since they are consumed faster than they are naturally produced.

Fuel cell: An electrochemical device in which hydrogen is combined with oxygen to produce electricity with heat and water-vapor as by-products. Natural gas is often used as the source of hydrogen, with air as the source of oxygen. Since electricity is produced by a chemical reaction and not by combustion, fuel cells are considered to be green power producers. Fuel-cell technology is quite old, dating back to the early days of the space program. Commercial use of fuel cells has been sporadic, although they are expected to be widely used in automobiles and buildings over the next decade.

g.

Global warming: An increase in the global mean temperature of the Earth that is (or is thought to be) a result of increased emissions of greenhouse gases trapped within the Earth's atmosphere. Global warming is believed to have adverse consequences such as climate change and a rise in sea levels. The scientific community is in general agreement that the Earth's surface has warmed by about 1° F in the past 140 years.

Gray water: Wastewater from sinks, showers, kitchens, washers, etc. Unlike black water, gray water does not contain human waste. After purification, gray water is typically used for non-potable purposes such as flushing and irrigation.

Green: A term that is widely used to describe a building and site designed in an environmentally sensitive manner (i.e., with minimal effect on the environment).

Green building: A building that minimizes impact on the environment through conservation of resources (energy, water, etc.) and contributes to the health of its occupants. Green buildings are characterized by comfortable and aesthetically pleasing environments.

Greenhouse effect: Greenhouse gases allow solar radiation to pass through the Earth's atmosphere, but prevent most of the reflected infrared radiation from the Earth's surface and lower atmosphere from escaping into outer space. This process occurs naturally and has kept the Earth's average surface temperature at approximately 60°F. Current life on Earth would not be possible without the natural greenhouse effect. Environmental scientists are concerned about the increased emissions of greenhouse gases from human activities, which can lead to climate change and its consequential adverse effects.

Greenhouse gases: Any gas that absorbs infrared radiation in the Earth's atmosphere. Common greenhouse gases include water vapor, carbon dioxide (CO_2), methane (CH_4), nitrogen oxides (NO_x), ozone (O_3), chlorofluorocarbons (CFCs), halogenated fluorocarbons (HCFCs), perfluorinated carbons (PFCs), hydrofluorocarbons (HFCs), and sulfur hexafluoride (SF_6). Carbon dioxide, methane, and nitrogen oxides are of particular concern because of their long residence time in the atmosphere.

Green power: Electricity generated from renewable energy sources (solar, wind, biomass, geothermal, and hydroelectric).

i.

Indoor air quality: The degree to which interior environments are free of known contaminants at harmful concentrations and a substantial majority of the people exposed to the air do not express dissatisfaction.

Insolation: The amount of sunlight (direct, diffuse, and reflected) reaching an area exposed to the sky.

k.

Kyoto Protocol: A legally binding agreement adopted by the countries in attendance at the December 1997 United Nations Framework Convention on Climate Change in Kyoto, Japan. Delegates from the 160 industrialized nations present agreed to reduce their greenhouse gas emissions by an average of 5.2 percent below 1990 emissions levels by 2010. The U.S. pledged a 7 percent reduction, although the U.S. Congress did not ratify the agreement.

l.

LEED: An acronym for Leadership in Energy and Environmental Design. LEED is a rating system developed by the U.S. Green Building Council to evaluate environmental performance from a whole-building perspective over a building's life cycle, providing a definitive standard for what constitutes a green building. Buildings are rated as green (certified), silver, gold, and platinum (highest level of green). Additional information can be found at www.usgbc.org.

Life-cycle cost: The cost of buying, operating, maintaining, and disposing of a system, equipment, product, or facility over its expected useful life.

Light shelf: A horizontal device usually positioned above eye level to reflect daylight onto the ceiling and beyond. A light shelf may project into a room, beyond an exterior wall plane, or both. The upper surface of the shelf is highly reflective (i.e., having 80 percent or greater reflectance). Light shelves are also effective shading devices for windows located below.

m.

Microclimate: Localized climate conditions within an urban area or building.

n.

Nitrogen oxides (NO_x): Gases consisting of one molecule of nitrogen and varying numbers of oxygen molecules. Nitrogen oxides are by-products of combustion processes and are commonly found in automobile exhaust and emissions from fossil fuel–fired power plants. NO_x is a greenhouse gas and an ingredient of acid rain and smog.

Nonrenewable energy resources: Energy resources that cannot be restored or replenished by natural processes and therefore are depleted through use. Commonly used nonrenewable resources include coal, oil, natural gas, and uranium.

o.

Orientation: The position of a building relative to the points of a compass. Energy consumption in a building can be reduced by proper orientation of the building's windows.

Ozone (O_3): Ozone is a greenhouse gas present in the stratosphere and the troposphere. In the stratosphere, ozone provides a protective layer that shields the Earth from harmful ultraviolet radiation. In the lower atmosphere, ozone is a pollutant that causes respiratory problems and is an ingredient of smog.

p.

Passive solar: The use of natural heat transfer processes to collect, distribute, and store usable heat without the help of mechanical devices such as pumps or fans. (Passive solar systems have few moving parts and are therefore "passive.") Trombe walls and the use of the thermal mass of a building's structure to store energy are both examples of passive solar systems.

Photovoltaic cell: A device that converts sunlight directly into electricity. Photovoltaic (PV) cells are silicon-based semiconductors and are often referred to as solar cells. Developed in the mid-1950s, they are cost-effective when it is difficult to extend conventional power lines. PV cells are often used for motorist call aid boxes, irrigation systems, and navigational lights.

r.

Rainwater harvesting: The collection, storage, and reuse of rainwater.

Recycling: A series of processes (including collection, separation, and processing) by which products and raw materials are recovered and reused in lieu of disposal as solid or liquid wastes. Commonly recycled items include cans and bottles, paper, and industrial solvents.

Regeneration: Renewal of sites or habitats that have become unfit for human, animal, or plant habitation to bring them back into productive use. The term is most commonly used to refer to urban and industrial land.

Renewable energy sources: Energy sources that replenish themselves naturally within a short period of time, including solar energy, hydroelectric power, geothermal energy, wind power, ocean thermal energy, and wave power.

R-value: A unit of thermal resistance. A material's R-value is a measure of the effectiveness of the material in stopping the flow of heat. The higher the R-value, the greater the material's insulating properties and the slower the heat flow through it.

s.

Shading coefficient: The ratio of solar heat gain through a glazing system to solar heat gain through a single layer of clear glass.

Sick Building syndrome: The Environmental Protection Agency and the National Institute of Occupational Safety and Health define Sick Building syndrome as "situations in which building occupants experience acute health and/or comfort effects that appear to be linked to time spent in a particular building, but where no specific illness or cause can be identified. The complaints may be localized in a particular room or zone, or may be spread throughout the building." Occupants experience relief of symptoms shortly after leaving the building.

Sustainability: The concept of sustainability can be traced back to President Theodore Roosevelt, who stated in 1910, "I recognize the right and duty of this generation to develop and use the natural resources of our land; but I do not recognize the right to waste them, or to rob, by wasteful use, the generations that come after us." In 1987, the United Nations World Commission on Environment and Development (the Bruntland Commission) defined a sustainable development as one that "meets the needs of the present without compromising the ability of future generations to meet their own needs." Sustainability has three interdependent dimensions relating to the environment, economics, and society—often referred to as the triple bottom line.

t.

Thermal mass: A material used to store heat, thereby slowing the temperature variation within a space. Typical thermal mass materials include concrete, brick, masonry, tile and mortar, water, and rock.

Triple bottom line: According to the World Business Council for Sustainable Development, "Sustainable development involves the simultaneous pursuit of economic prosperity, environmental quality, and social equity. Companies aiming for sustainability need to perform not against a single, financial bottom line, but against [this] triple bottom line."

v.

Volatile organic compound (VOC): An organic compound that evaporates at room temperature and is often hazardous to human health, causing poor indoor air quality. Sources of VOCs include solvents and paints. Many materials commonly used in building construction (such as carpets, furniture, and paints) emit VOCs.

Bibliography

General Reference Books

Abley, Ian, and James Heartfield, eds. *Sustaining Architecture in the Anti-Machine Age*. Chichester, England: Wiley-Academic, 2001.

————

Banham, Reyner. *The Architecture of the Well-Tempered Environment*. London: Architectural P., 1969.

Battle, Guy, and Christopher McCarthy. *Sustainable Ecosystems and the Built Environment*. Chichester, England: John Wiley & Sons, 2001.

Behling, Sophia and Stefan. *Glass: Structure and Technology in Architecture*. New York: Prestel, 1999.

Behling, Sophia and Stefan. *Solar Power: The Evolution of Sustainable Architecture*. New York: Prestel, 2000.

Beukers, Adriaan, and Ed van Hinte. *Lightness: The Inevitable Renaissance of Minimum Energy Structures*. Rotterdam: 010 Publishers, 1998.

————

Campi, Mario. *Skyscrapers: An Architectural Type of Modern Urbanism*. Basel, Boston, and Berlin: Birkhauser, 2000.

————

Earth Pledge Foundation. *Sustainable Architecture White Papers*. New York: Earth Pledge Foundation, 2001.

————

Ferriss, Hugh. *Metropolis of Tomorrow*. New York: I. Washburn, 1929. Reprint. New York: Princeton Architectural Press, 1986.

Fry, Maxwell, and Jane Drew. *Tropical Architecture in the Dry and Humid Zones*. New York: Reinhold Pub. Corp., 1964.

————

Herzog, Thomas. *Solar Energy in Architecture and Urban Planning*. Munich and New York: Prestel, 1996.

————

Jones, David Lloyd. *Architecture and the Environment: Bioclimatic Building Design*. London: Laurence King, 1998.

————

Kunstler, James Howard. *The City in Mind: Meditations on the Urban Condition*. New York: Free Press, 2001.

Landau, Sarah Bradford, and Carl W. Condit. *Rise of the New York Skyscraper, 1865–1913*. New Haven: Yale University Press, 1996.

————

Matthews, Emily. *The Weight of Nations: Material Outflows from Industrial Economies*. Washington, DC: World Resources Institute, 2000.

McDonough, William, and Michael Braungart. *Cradle to Cradle: Remaking the Way We Make Things*. New York: North Point Press, 2002.

Melet, Ed. *Sustainable Architecture: Towards a Diverse Built Environment*. Rotterdam: NAI Publishers, 1999.

Mendler, Sarah, and Bill Odell. *The HOK Guidebook to Sustainable Design*. New York: John Wiley & Sons, 2000.

————

Norman, Donald. *The Design of Everyday Things*. New York: Doubleday, 1990.

————

Olgyay, Victor. *Design with Climate: Bioclimatic Approach to Architectural Regionalism*. Princeton: Princeton University Press, 1963.

————

Rogers, Richard. *Cities for a Small Planet*. London: Faber & Faber, 1997.

————

Scott, Andrew. *Dimensions of Sustainability*. London and New York: E & FN Spon, 1998.

Slessor, Catherine. *Eco-Tech: Sustainable Architecture and High Technology*. New York: Thames and Hudson, 1997.

Steele, James. *Sustainable Architecture: Principles, Paradigms, and Case Studies*. New York: McGraw-Hill, 1997.

————

Wines, James. *Green Architecture*. New York: Taschen, 2000.

————

Yeang, Kenneth, *The Green Skyscraper: The Basis for Designing Sustainable Intensive Buildings*. New York: Prestel, 1999.

Books about Featured Architects and Buildings

Ban, Shigeru. *Shigeru Ban*. New York: Princeton Architectural Press, 2001.

Blaser, Werner. *Ingenhoven Overdiek Kahlen und Partner: Architects High-Rise RWE AG Essen*. Berlin and Boston: Birkhauser, 2000.

———

Croxton Collaborative. *Audubon House: Building the Environmentally Responsible, Energy-Efficient Office*. New York: John Wiley & Sons, 1994.

———

Davies, Colin. *Hopkins 2: The Work of Michael Hopkins and Partners*. London: Phaidon Press, 2001.

Dobney, Stephen. *Norman Foster: Selected and Current Works of Foster and Partners*. Victoria, Australia: Images Pub. Group, 1999.

Doubilet, Susan. *Fox & Fowle*. Milan: l'Arca Edizioni, 2000.

———

Feireiss, Kristin. *Ingenhoven Overdiek and Partner: Energies*. Berlin and Boston: Birkhauser, 2002.

Flagge, Ingeborg. *Thomas Herzog: Architecture and Technology*. New York: Prestel USA, 2002.

———

Herzog, Thomas. *Expodach: Roof Structure at the World Exhibition, Hanover 2000*. New York: Prestel USA, 2000.

Herzog, Thomas. *Sustainable Height Deutschemesse AG Hanover*. New York: Prestel USA, 2000.

———

Ingenhoven, Christof. *Ingenhoven Overdiek and Partner: Architects 1991–1999*. Cambridge: Birkhauser, 2000.

———

Jenkins, David, ed. *On Foster — Foster On*. Munich and New York: Prestel, 2000.

Kohn Pedersen Fox. *Kohn Pedersen Fox*. Victoria, Australia: Images Pub. Group, 1998.

Kohn, Wendy. *Moshe Safdie*. London: John Wiley & Sons, 1996.

Kronenburg, Robert. *Future Tents Limited (FTL) Architects: Softness, Movement, and Light*. Chichester, England: Lanham, MD, 1997.

———

MVRDV. *Farmax: Excursions on Density*. Rotterdam: 010 Publishers, 1998.

———

National Audubon Society. *Audubon Headquarters: Building for an Environmental Future*. New York: National Audubon Society, 1991.

———

Pawley, Martin, and Norman Foster. *Norman Foster: A Global Architecture*. New York: St. Martin's Press, 1999.

Perkins & Will. *Perkins & Will: Selected and Current Works*. Victoria, Australia: Images Pub. Group, 2001.

Powell, Kenneth. *Richard Rogers: Complete Works*. New York: Phaidon Press, 2001.

Powell, Robert. *Re-thinking the Skyscraper: The Complete Architecture of Kenneth Yeang*. New York: Whitney Library of Design, 1999.

———

Rogers, Richard. *Richard Rogers Architects*. New York: St. Martin's Press, 1986.

———

Whyte, Andy. *Skidmore, Owings & Merrill: Architecture and Urbanism, 1995–2000*. Victoria, Australia: Images Pub. Group, 2001.

Acknowledgments

The exhibition team thanks the authors who contributed to an exciting overview of recent sustainable design practices in *Big & Green*. William McDonough's preface set the bar for the discussions within the catalog. Guy Battle, Michael Braungart, David Serlin, and James Wines developed insightful texts that will influence future discussion of the subject. Ashok Raiji's glossary helps clarify many of the terms used within the movement. Nina Rappaport's work interviewing William Browning, Bruce Fowle, Robert Fox, Richard Rogers, and Kenneth Yeang gave the catalog a practitioners' perspective that would otherwise be missing. The interviewees were generous in making themselves available and in providing their thoughts on the practice of sustainable architecture.

The design of the catalog is the product of the combined talents of Paul Carlos and Urshula Barbour at Pure+Applied. In the exhibition design, Pure+Applied benefited immensely from the design talent of James Hicks. Noel Millea edited the catalog's content and helped determine its overall arguments. Mark Lamster and Kevin Lippert of Princeton Architectural Press believed in the project from the start and patiently saw the catalog through to completion.

Big & Green benefitted from the assistance of the principals and employees of the exhibited architecture firms. In particular, the exhibition team wishes to thank the following individuals for their enormous devotion of time and materials: Guy Battle, Guy Lafayette, and Robert Thomas of Battle McCarthy Consulting Engineers & Landscape Architects; Mig Halpine of Cesar Pelli & Associates; Douglas Kot and Randall Croxton of the Croxton Collaborative; Kendall Wilson of Envision Design; Elizabeth Walker and Katy Harris of Foster and Partners; Kirsten Sibilia of Fox & Fowle Architects; Tom Onay of FTL Design Engineering Studio; Mara Baum of Hellmuth, Obata + Kassabaum; Bunthit Rajtboriraks and Chris Gordon of Kishimoto.Gordon; Ute Einhoff of Ingenhoven Overdiek und Partner; Gregory Kiss and Gabrielle Brainard of Kiss + Cathcart Architects; A. Eugene Kohn and Ilona Rider of Kohn Pedersen Fox Associates; Rebecca Chipchase of Michael Hopkins and Partners; Anna Moca of Morphosis; Moshe Safdie and Elise Youn of Moshe Safdie and Associates; Odette Bruinzeel of MVRDV; Sally Kennedy of Nicholas Grimshaw and Partners; Mick Pearce of the Pearce Partnership; Yvonne Szeto of PEI COBB FREED + PARTNERS Architects; Ralph Johnson of Perkins & Will; Lucy Dean and Robert Torday of the Richard Rogers Partnership; Ellen Dougherty of Rafael Viñoly Architects; Peter Dixon of Robert A.M. Stern Architects; Malcolm McGowan of Sheppard Robson; Tetsuya Matsuyama of Shigeru Ban; Denise Lee and James Wines of SITE Projects, Inc.; Elizabeth Kubany of Skidmore, Owings & Merrill; Peter Testa; Kenneth Yeang of T.R. Hamzah and Yeang; and Kyle Copas of William McDonough + Partners.

Material provided by these firms was supplemented by the following archives, institutions, and photographers, who provided access to their collections and assistance in locating images: Robert Davies, Judith Arthur, Christian Richters, Erica Stoller, Peter Aaron, Jeff Goldberg, Ian Lambot, Michael Moran, Richard Bryant, Otto Baitz, Michael Lent, Dieter Liestner, Daniela MacAdden, H.G. Esch, Holger Knauf, Duane Lempke, Eamonn O'Mahony, Michal Safdie, Hans Werlemann, David Brazier, Luc Boegly, Bruce White, John Donat, Peter Cook, Dennis Gilbert, John Linden, Jay Langlois, Mark Luthringer, Kenneth Willardt, Daniel Aubry, David Sunberg, Norman McGrath, Kriz Kizak Wines, the Frank Lloyd Wright Foundation, the Cooper-Hewitt National Design Museum, the Regional Plan Association of New York, Krieger Publishing, the Chicago Historical Society, and Yale University.

Many of the ideas in the exhibition are the result of input from the exhibition cochairs, Jeffrey Abramson, Douglas Durst, and A. Eugene Kohn, and members of the advisory council, Betty Arndt, William Browning, Randall Croxton, Bruce Fowle, Robert Fox, Kriz Kizak Wines, William McDonough, William Odell, Ashok Raiji, Gerald Sigal, Kendall Wilson, and James Wines.

Product manufacturers and their representatives were enormously generous with time and materials. Jerry Paner of BP Solar, Betty Arndt and Paul von Paumgartten of Johnson Controls, and Steven Strong helped us understand how various products function and appreciate their role in sustainable design.

At the National Building Museum, we wish to thank the Board of Trustees and president Susan Henshaw Jones, who realized the project by coordinating the various curatorial, educational, and fund-raising initiatives. Howard Decker, chief curator, participated in the initial conception of the project and has provided consistent support of the exhibition and catalog. Martin Moeller, senior vice president for special projects, reviewed the catalog material and provided helpful comments at every stage of development. Jennifer Bertsch, executive assistant and manager of board relations, helped coordinate the various meetings and reviews for the exhibition and catalog. Essence Newhoff, director of development for exhibitions, worked on the project from the beginning and contributed many important ideas for its content. Together with Julie Wolf-Rodda, vice president for development, they made the exhibition and catalog possible through research and the difficult work of fund-raising. Jennifer Byrne, publications designer, and Jill Dixon, director of public affairs, developed the brochures and other public materials for the exhibition. Ed Worthy, vice president for education, provided helpful comments throughout the planning process and, with Christina Wilson, director of public programs, and Paul Killmer, public programs coordinator, developed the lectures for the exhibition and other public programs. Mike Nelson, senior vice president for finance and administration, patiently and enthusiastically pushed the project forward at several key moments. Curators Chrysanthe Broikos and Mary Konsoulis reviewed the catalog introduction and developed ideas that were critical to its arguments. Cecelia Gibson, exhibition registrar, and Dana Twersky, collections manager, made themselves available for help in acquiring objects. Hank Griffith, exhibitions coordinator, Chris Maclay, exhibitions preparator, and Elizabeth Kaleida, exhibition designer and preparator, provided assistance with the exhibition's design and fabrication.

Finally, a number of colleagues, former instructors, and other individuals provided expertise and wrote letters for grants. The exhibition team wishes to thank Raymond Gastil, Dolores Hayden, and Robert A.M. Stern for their early support in the museum's successful application to the Graham Foundation for Advanced Studies in the Fine Arts. Along with Bob Bruegmann and Kenneth Frampton, they helped shape the project's direction. Paul Stoller of Atelier 10, Catherine Slessor of the *Architectural Review*, and Stefan and Sofia Behling of Foster and Partners provided technical data and helpful connections to various people.

Catherine Frankel
David Gissen
Alisa Goetz

Index of Architecture Firms

Photo Credits

PAGE 10: (left) Joseph Sohm, ChromoSohm Inc./Corbis; (right) Richard Davies. PAGE 11: (far left) courtesy New York Historical Society; (left) Norman McGrath; (middle and right) Norman McGrath. PAGE 12: (left) Cathy Kelly; (right) Donald Corner. PAGE 13: (left) courtesy Foster and Partners; (right) Richard Bryant/Arcaid. PAGE 14: (left) Otto Baitz; (middle) Frederick Charles; (right) Frederick Charles. PAGE 15: K. L. Ng Photography. PAGE 16: Jeff Goldberg/Esto. PAGE 17: (left) Hans Werlemann; (right) Ian Lambot/Arcaid. PAGE 21: Nigel Young. PAGES 22–23: Jeff Goldberg/Esto. PAGE 25: David Sundberg. PAGE 31: Eamonn O'Mahony. PAGE 32: Jock Pottle/Esto. PAGES 34–35: Eamonn O'Mahony. PAGE 36: courtesy NASA. PAGE 38: Imagebank. PAGE 42: Ian Lambot/Arcaid. (All other photographs in "The Air We Breathe" courtesy Battle McCarthy Consulting Engineers & Landscape Architects.) PAGE 48: (top left) Mortiz Korn; (all others) Dieter Leistner. PAGE 49: Dieter Leistner. PAGES 50–51: Daniela Mac Adden. PAGE 52: Holger Knauf. PAGE 53: H.G. Esch, Hennef. PAGES 54–55: Duane Lempke/Fifson Studios. PAGES 56–57: Eamonn O'Mahony. PAGES 58–59: Richard Davies. PAGES 62–63: David Brazier. PAGE 64: Scagliola/Brakkee. PAGE 65: Luc Boegly/Archipress. PAGES 70–71: Peter Aaron. PAGE 72: courtesy Sheppard Robson. PAGE 73: (Helicon) Richard Bryant/Arcaid. PAGE 74: Steinkamp Ballogg. PAGES 76–77: K. L. Ng Photography. PAGE 78: Bettmann/Corbis. PAGE 79: Richard Cummins/Corbis. PAGE 80: (left) Francis G. Mayer/Corbis; (middle) Neil Beer/Corbis; (right) David Samuel Robbins/Corbis. PAGE 81: (left) Thomas A. Heinz/Corbis; (middle) Corbis; (right) Frank Lloyd Wright Foundation, Scottsdale, Arizona. PAGE 82: Frank Lloyd Wright Foundation, Scottsdale, Arizona. PAGE 83: Corbis. PAGE 84: Timothy Hursley. (All other photographs in "Vertiscapes" courtesy SITE Projects, Inc.) PAGES 84–85: Ian Lambot/Arcaid. PAGES 92–93: Richard Davies. PAGES 94–95: Hans Werlemann. PAGES 98–99: Richard Bryant/Arcaid. PAGE 101: Apex. PAGE 103: (top) courtesy SITE Projects, Inc.; (bottom) Peter Aaron/Esto. PAGES 104–5: (Avenue V) Daniel Aubry. PAGES 106–7: K. L. Ng Photography. PAGES 108–9: K. L. Ng Photography. PAGES 110–11: Mark Luthringer. PAGE 114: Tim Griffith/Esto. PAGE 115: Stephanie Maze/Corbis. PAGE 116: (left) Wayne Andrews/Esto; (middle) Esto; (right) Corbis. PAGE 117: (left) Peter Aaron/Esto; (right) Arcaid. PAGE 118: (left) Reuters NewMedia Inc./Corbis; (right) Norman McGrath. PAGE 119: (left) Daniela Mac Adden; (right) Otto Baitz. PAGES 120–21: Jeff Goldberg/Esto. PAGE 123: (left) Photodisk; (right) courtesy BASF. PAGE 124: courtesy Colbi Brett Cannon. PAGE 125: Barney Taxel. PAGES 128–29: Otto Baitz. PAGES 130–31: Michael Moran. PAGE 135: Michal Safdie. PAGE 136: (top) Janet Gill; (middle left) Peter Cook; (all others) Richard Bryant/Arcaid. PAGE 137: Richard Bryant/Arcaid. PAGE 139: Eamonn O'Mahony. PAGES 140–41: Christian Richters/Fotograf. PAGE 142: Peter Testa. PAGE 143: Jeffrey Tsui. PAGE 144: AFP/Corbis. PAGE 147: Roger Ressmeyer/Corbis. PAGE 149: (left) Johnson Controls Inc. PAGE 150: Buffalo and Erie County Historical Society. PAGE 151: (left) Mishima; (right) Richard Bryant/Arcaid. PAGE 152: Richard Davies. PAGE 153: Corbis. PAGE 156: courtesy Cesar Pelli & Associates. PAGES 158–59: courtesy Foster and Partners. PAGE 160: Timothy Hursley. PAGE 161: (middle) Jock Pottle/Esto; (all others) Timothy Hursley. PAGES 164–65: Eamonn O'Mahony. PAGES 166–68: K.L. Ng Photography.

Colophon

DESIGN & TYPOGRAPHY
Paul Carlos & Urshula Barbour | Pure+Applied

TYPEFACES & SETTING
This book was set using
ITC Conduit (Mark Van Bronkhorst, 1997) and
FF Typestar (Steffen Sauerteig, 1996)
on QuarkXpress 4.0

Printed and bound in China.